Geography
ACTIVITIES

Author

Sarah D. Giese

SHELL EDUCATION

Contributing Authors to Introduction
Garth Sundem, M.M.
Kristi A. Pikiewica

Editor
Walter Kelly, M.A.

Project Manager
Gillian Eve Makepeace

Editorial Director
Emily R. Smith, M.A.Ed.

Editor-in-Chief
Sharon Coan, M.S.Ed.

Editorial Manager
Gisela Lee, M.A.

Creative Director
Lee Aucoin

Illustration Manager/Illustrator
Timothy J. Bradley

Cover Artist
Lesley Palmer

Cover Art
Corel

Production Manager
Peter Pulido

Imaging
Phil Garcia
Misty Shaw

Standards
National Council for Geographic
Education, 1994
Compendium, Copyright 2004 McREL

Publisher
Corinne Burton, M.A.Ed.

Acknowledgments

Jennifer Farlow, Blalack Middle School, Carrollton-Farmers Branch Independent School District,
    Carrollton, Texas
Judy Freeman, Kenmore Middle School, Arlington Public Schools, Arlington, Virginia
John Hart, Swanson Middle School, Arlington Public Schools, Arlington, Virginia
Gail Humphries Mardirosian, Imagination Quest Team Leader: Imagination Quest, an arts-based
    teaching/learning model at Imagination Stage, American University, Washington, D.C.
Diana Jordan, Kenmore Middle School, Arlington Public Schools, Arlington, Virginia
Linda Overholser, Coal Creek Elementary School, Boulder Valley School District,
    Louisville, Colorado
Eric Tarquinio, Swanson Middle School, Arlington Public Schools, Arlington, Virginia

Shell Education
5301 Oceanus Drive
Huntington Beach, CA 92649-1030
http://www.shelleducation.com
ISBN 978-1-4258-0383-4
© 2006 by Shell Educational Publishing, Inc.
Reprinted 2012

Table of Contents

Introduction

It was hard to carry water from the bucket to the cup at my desk because my desk was far away, and that's why people wanted to live close to rivers. Also it was easier to work as a group than on your own because you could work together and get free time for art and inventing stuff, and that's why people formed societies.

—Sixth grade student in Bozeman, Montana

Benefits of Hands-on Learning

Research is now validating what teachers have known intuitively all along: hands-on learning increases retention and understanding.

Using both history and political science classes, the studies found that students who participated in the role-plays and collaborative exercises did better on subsequent standard evaluations than their traditionally instructed peers (McCarthy and Anderson 2000).

For example, students at a St. Louis middle school experimenting with hands-on learning methods have scored consistently higher on the Stanford Achievement Tests than those in other district schools (Harvey, Sirna, and Houlihan 1998). In other words, once a student has built the Great Wall of China out of salt dough, he or she will remember it forever. By linking learning with experience, we encourage students to remember information as part of this action.

In addition to increasing assessment scores, hands-on learning also increases student motivation. "Tactile learning activities generated positive evaluative attitudes in fifth-grade learners toward geography. These learners did better academically when their competence was measured by content tests" (Blahut and Nicely 1984). Students enjoy hands-on activities, and when students are motivated, they learn.

Though still new to the world of social studies, hands-on learning is not revolutionary in all teaching disciplines. Science teachers use an increasingly hands-on, experimental approach in their teaching.

Benefits of Hands-on Learning *(cont.)*

Jean Piaget (1986) said the following about the need for a shift toward experimental learning in science education:

> A sufficient experimental training was believed to have been provided as long as the student had been introduced to the results of past experiments or had been allowed to watch demonstration experiments conducted by his teacher, as though it were possible to sit in rows on a wharf and learn to swim merely by watching grown-up swimmers in the water . . . the repetition of past experiments is still a long way from being the best way of exciting the spirit of invention . . .

It is in hopes of exciting the spirit of invention that we offer this book of social studies simulations. More precisely, these simulations and games are designed to excite the spirit of exploration, providing both the experiential basis of knowledge and also the spark of interest so needed to encourage further study. For example, while gaining an overview of a historic period through simulated daily life, students may also be competing as small groups to conquer neighboring groups. These games are cool in much the same way that a snowball fight is cool. By making your subject cool you immediately trick students into intellectual excitement and curiosity. For many teachers in the early and middle grades, sparking this excitement in later study is a goal unto itself.

Piaget also says that involvement is the key to intellectual development. Using these games, you will involve all students, each at their differentiated level of ability and each in their preferred method of learning. For example, in the course of an activity, you may split your class into small groups in which one student makes group decisions, another interacts with neighboring groups, other students are delegated to read background material and talk with their partners, while the remaining students work to complete hands-on design and construction projects. These classroom-tested simulations involve all five of your students' senses and allow students to choose the learning styles that are best for them.

The included simulations also offer many opportunities for small group interaction, encouraging a collaborative approach to learning, which is yet another strategy validated by research. "Total reading, language, mathematics, and battery scores indicated that students in the cooperative learning class scored higher than students in the traditional class" (Pratt and Moesner 1990).

Benefits of Hands-on Learning *(cont.)*

Today is an exciting time in social studies education. More and more we are creating authentic experiences for our students, be they through simulations, active learning, or even evaluation of primary source materials. We are coming to respect that it is more powerful for students to walk through the rows of crosses at Arlington National Cemetery than it is to read the words of a historian. We see that exploring African American sheet music of the 1850s as archived by the American Memory Project at the Library of Congress creates a much more personal response to segregation in American history than simply discussing the issue as a class.

We hope this book helps you infuse your classroom with the light of discovery and learning, allows you to add richness to your students' experiences, and helps you show students that history is not dead. Social studies is alive, breathing, and evolving, and not only in a laboratory or research facility, but in your classroom. People today are part of the same culture and the web of history connects us all. Through experiencing and appreciating the goals, struggles, and decisions of past societies, students in your classroom will gain a deeper appreciation for the world-changing issues facing people today.

Geography Information

In an increasingly interconnected world, it is vital that young Americans know and understand not only where places are located, but why they are there and how the people who live there interact with their environments. These principles form the core of geography education. Statistics have shown for years that American students lag far behind their counterparts in other countries in the area of geographic knowledge.

The activities in this book are divided into three sections: geography skills, physical geography, and cultural geography. These divisions represent the major emphases of geography. While it is important that our students learn to develop and use geography skills, it is just as important that they learn to apply those skills to Earth's natural and human characteristics. Geography is not just about "Where"—it is also about "Why."

Geography Information *(cont.)*

The geography skills section introduces your students to the basics of geography. In this section, your students will compare different ways of examining the world. They will learn to identify various land and water forms. They will investigate map components and their purposes. They will study map projections. And, they will find and use latitude and longitude. These skills form the backbone of any geography curriculum and will give your students the capacity and confidence to dive into the world of geography.

The physical geography section leads your students to explore the physical, or natural, world. Physical geography encompasses those parts of Earth that can exist without humans—climate, vegetation, plate tectonics, water, and natural disasters. Your students will investigate how Earth and its physical systems work.

The cultural geography section focuses on human geography—all the aspects of geography concerned with people. A place is defined not only by its physical characteristics but also by its human characteristics. In this section, you will find activities on cultural identity, economics, politics, architecture, and human-environment interaction to pique your students' interest in cultural geography.

The concluding activity (final project) is designed to unify the application of geography skills, understanding of physical geography, and appreciation for aspects of cultural geography. Focus is directed toward one country and asks the students to bring together their academic knowledge and skills in a creative activity to synthesize what has been learned.

Arts Integration

Arts integration helps bring the geography activities in this book to life. Integrating arts into a geography curriculum adds a dimension of creativity and self-expression for students. As Mantione and Smead (2003) note in their work with integrating arts to teach reading comprehension:

> The arts require everyone to interact with their whole selves, thereby engendering the intellectual passion we so dearly want for all children. Teaching reading comprehension strategies through the arts is an approach that is an inclusive, multidimensional, passionate experience.

Arts Integration *(cont.)*

This same experience can be encountered in these geography activities. Whether students are performing raps that explain the causes and effects of human-environment interaction or acting out the consequences of plate tectonics on the physical environment, the activities outlined here access students' innate excitement for learning. The activities included in this book all strive to incorporate several different art forms. A brief description of each art form is included to help the teacher integrate the arts in meaningful ways.

Arts integration also lends itself to Howard Gardner's theory of Multiple Intelligences. Below is a chart that illustrates which arts integration activities address which intelligences. All of the activities in this book include numerous stages, and those stages can also be tied to Gardner's intelligences. This chart addresses only the arts component of each activity.

Multiple Intelligence	Geography Topic
Logical	Land and Water Forms; Plate Tectonics; Political Systems; Natural Disasters
Visual	Map Skills; Economics; Cultural Identity; Latitude and Longitude; Architecture
Spatial	Land and Water Forms; Political Systems; Natural Disasters
Body/Kinesthetic	Land and Water Forms; Climate; Plate Tectonics; Global Water Issues
Musical/Rhythmic	Latitude and Longitude; Vegetation; Human-Environment Interaction
Intrapersonal	Land and Water Forms; Vegetation; Architecture; Natural Disasters; Cultural Identity; Political Systems
Interpersonal	Map Skills; Latitude and Longitude; Climate; Plate Tectonics; Economics; Human-Environment Interaction; Natural Disasters; Global Water Issues
Naturalist	The arts components are not specifically for the naturalist learners, but the subject itself, especially physical geography, engages these learners.

Works Cited

Blahut, John M., and Robert F. Nicely Jr. 1984. Tactile activities and learning attitudes. *Social Education* 48: 153–158.

Gardner, Howard. 1983. *Frames of mind: The theory of multiple intellingences*. New York: BasicBooks.

Harvey, Barbara Z.; Richard T. Sirna; Margaret B. Houlihan. 1998. Learning by design: Hands-on learning. *American School Board Journal* 186: 22–25.

Mantione, Roberta D. and Sabine Smead. 2003. *Weaving through words: Using the arts to teach reading comprehension strategies.* Newark: International Reading Association.

McCarthy, J. Patrick and Liam Anderson. 2000. Active learning techniques versus traditional teaching styles: Two experiments from history and political science. *Innovative Higher Education* 24: 279–294.

Piaget, Jean. 1986. Essay on necessity. *Human Development* 29: 301–314.

Pratt, Sherry J. and Cheryl Moesner. 1990. A comparative study of traditional and cooperative learning on student achievement. ERIC database #325258.

Overview of Activities

Land and Water Forms *(pages 12–16)*

Fantasy Island—In this activity, students learn to differentiate land and water features. Students start by labeling blank maps of imaginary lands. Then, they play charades to reinforce their knowledge of land and water forms. Finally, they create their own fantasy islands using these features.

Map Components *(pages 17–23)*

Which Way to the Pencil Sharpener?—In this lesson, students define map components and examine their uses. Students first examine a map of a known area, such as their school, making conclusions about map components. Then, students create maps on their own and use those maps to complete treasure hunts.

Map Projections *(pages 24–37)*

Perspective Detectives—In this activity, students take photographs of familiar objects in unfamiliar ways, analyze photographs taken by other students, and examine several old maps to hypothesize about their purposes and perspectives. Finally, students create maps of their classroom using their unique photographs from the beginning of the activity.

Latitude and Longitude *(pages 38–55)*

Grid and Bear It!—In this activity, students learn to use latitude and longitude to identify absolute location. Students will read a brief introduction, diagram and act out latitude and longitude, play a version of the old game *Battleship* to reinforce their knowledge, and create books to help them remember the process of finding latitude and longitude.

Read, Read, Read Your Map—In this activity, students review the process of finding latitude and longitude of a location by working in pairs, practice finding latitude and longitude by "hunting" for their teacher, and strengthen their knowledge by creating songs about latitude and longitude.

Climate *(pages 56–70)*

Weather or Not—In this lesson, students learn the factors that determine an area's climate and how to read a climate graph. They use this knowledge to identify major cities based on their climates and create tableaux to demonstrate major climate patterns and how they relate to location.

Vegetation *(pages 71–80)*

Growing Pains—Students investigate the ties between climate patterns and vegetation. They plant crops to reinforce their knowledge and to infer implications for global hunger. Finally, they create acrostic poems explaining climate patterns and vegetation in their own words.

Plate Tectonics *(pages 81–85)*

Rock Your World—Students investigate four types of plate movement—convergence, divergence, subduction, and faulting—using a puzzle and class readings. Then, students use simple movement to create skits of plate movement and its effects on the physical environment. (*This lesson was created by Diana Jordan of Kenmore Middle School in Arlington, Virginia.*)

Natural Disasters *(pages 86–102)*

There's Trouble Brewin'—Students identify the causes and effects of various natural disasters and how humans adapt to places susceptible to these events. Students create trading cards of natural disasters and play a game to collect a complete set of cards.

Global Water Issues *(pages 103–117)*

Water, Water, Everywhere—In this activity, students analyze the importance of fresh water to everyday life. Students take a virtual tour of some of the world's water-stressed areas, answer questions about access and availability, and then create news reports.

Cultural Identity *(pages 118–127)*

Culture Quest—In this activity, students explore the factors that determine people's cultural identities. Students compare and contrast languages and religions, after which they create and perform monologues for characters from other cultures.

Economics *(pages 128–138)*

Money Makes the World Go 'Round—In this activity, students analyze the connections between physical geography and the ways that people make money. They research physical and economic characteristics of a country and engage in an auction to draw conclusions about geography and economics.

Political Systems *(pages 139–150)*

Who's in Charge?—In this activity, students investigate the main types of government and compare how power is distributed in each system by experiencing life under each type of system. Then, they create mobiles of the different types of governments.

Architecture *(pages 151–155)*

Home Sweet Home—Students examine photographs on the Web of architecture from around the globe and analyze examples of how architecture reflects the physical geography of a region. Then, they engage in a creative writing activity to synthesize their knowledge.

Human-Environment Interaction *(pages 156–166)*

Balancing Act—Small groups study specific types of human-environment interaction (HEI) and then create raps about the causes and effects of HEI.

Final Project *(pages 167–173)*

Countries, They're GRRRReat! In this final project, students create cereal boxes advertising the countries of their choice, using principles of advertising art and the skills from this series. Their projects will reflect the physical and cultural geography of their chosen countries.

Correlation to Standards

Standards Used in This Product

Shell Education (SEP) is committed to producing educational materials that are research and standards based. In this effort, the company uses the Mid-continent Research for Education and Learning (McREL) Standards Compendium. Each year, McREL analyzes state standards and revises the compendium. By following this procedure, McREL produces a general compilation of national standards. Each lesson in this book is based on a McREL standard. Then, the product is correlated to the academic standards of all 50 states, the District of Columbia, and the Department of Defense Dependent Schools. You can print a correlation report customized for your state directly from the SEP website at **http://www.seppub.com**. For assistance in printing correlation reports, please contact Customer Service at 1-877-777-3450.

Lesson Title	McREL Geography Standard
Fantasy Island	Knows the location of places, geographic features, and patterns of the environment. (Standard 2)
Which Way to the Pencil Sharpener?	Understands the characteristics and uses of maps, globes, and other geographic tools and technologies. (Standard 1)
Perspective Detectives	Understands the characteristics and uses of maps, globes, and other geographic tools and technologies. (Standard 1)
Grid and Bear It!	Understands the characteristics and uses of maps, globes, and other geographic tools and technologies. (Standard 1); Understands the characteristics and uses of spatial organization of Earth's surface. (Standard 3)
Read, Read, Read Your Map	Understands the characteristics and uses of maps, globes, and other geographic tools and technologies. (Standard 1)
Weather or Not	Understands the characteristics of ecosystems on Earth's surface. (Standard 8)
Growing Pains	Understands the characteristics of ecosystems on Earth's surface. (Standard 8)
Rock Your World	Knows the physical processes that shape patterns on Earth's surface. (Standard 7)
There's Trouble Brewin'	Knows the physical processes that shape patterns on Earth's surface. (Standard 7)
Water, Water, Everywhere	Understands the characteristics of ecosystems on Earth's surface. (Standard 8)
Culture Quest	Understands the nature and complexity of Earth's cultural mosaics. (Standard 10)
Money Makes the World Go 'Round	Understands the patterns and networks of economic interdependence on Earth's surface. (Standard 11)
Who's in Charge?	Understands the forces of cooperation and conflict that shape the divisions of Earth's surface. (Standard 13)
Home Sweet Home	Understands how physical systems affect human systems. (Standard 15)
Balancing Act	Understands how human actions modify the physical environment (Standard 14); Understands how physical systems affect human systems. (Standard 15)
Countries, They're GRRRReat!	Understands the physical and human characteristics of place. (Standard 4)

Fantasy Island

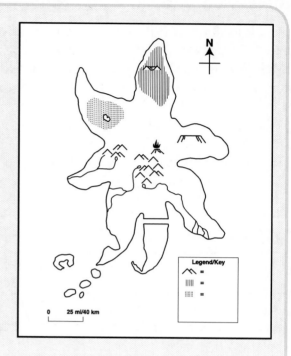

Overview

In this activity, students learn to differentiate among various land and water features. Students start by labeling a blank map of an imaginary land, then they play charades to reinforce their knowledge of various land and water forms, and finally they create their own fantasy islands using those various features.

The answer key for student reproducibles is located at the end of the lesson. It is helpful for the teacher to examine such keys before beginning the lesson or distributing any reproducibles to the class. This type of advance inspection will (1) improve teacher understanding and presentation, (2) prepare the teacher for possible alternative student responses, (3) help with classroom time management, and (4) result in optimum focus and effectiveness for the activity.

Objective

- Students will know the location of places, geographic features, and patterns of the environment.

Central Question

How do physical features relate to each other?

Materials

You will need to prepare and/or provide the following:

- *Physical Map of Fantasy Island* (1 per student), page 14
- overhead transparency of *Physical Map of Fantasy Island*, page 14
- overhead transparency of *Feature Cards*, page 15

- class set of *Feature Cards*
- green and blue construction paper (optional)
- blank paper
- crayons, markers, etc.

Answer Key

Physical Map of Fantasy Island Key . . . . .page 16

Fantasy Island *(cont.)*

Directions

Day One

1. Pass out one copy of the *Physical Map of Fantasy Island* to each student, and project the overhead transparency of the *Feature Cards*.

2. Students can use the terms on the *Feature Cards* to label as many features as they can on their maps. As they work, they should add to the map legend. Give them about ten minutes to do this. You may wish to have them use pencils to make corrections easier.

3. Call on volunteers to label the features of the overhead transparency of the island. When your volunteers are finished, help the class fill in any remaining blanks.

4. Answer any questions your students have about the differences between features. For example, students are commonly confused about the difference between a harbor and a bay (a harbor is human-made, while a bay is natural) or between a bay and a gulf (gulfs are larger).

Day Two

1. Before class, cut out a class set of the *Feature Cards*. (*Optional:* Glue them onto color-coded construction paper. Use green for land features and blue for water features.)

2. *Arts Integration:* Shuffle the *Feature Cards* and give one to each student. Tell them not to share with their neighbors. Explain the rules of charades to the class (no talking; use only gestures to convey the ideas; hold up fingers for the number of syllables in their features; etc.). Your students will act out the features on their cards, and the rest of the class must guess what features are being represented. They can use their completed *Physical Maps of Fantasy Island* as reference. The student who correctly guesses each feature gets to choose the next player.

3. It may be helpful to your students for you to model charades for them. Keep one *Feature Card* for yourself so that you can act it out for them.

4. If you choose to use colored-paper backgrounds, have students hold up the backs of their *Feature Cards* before they begin their charades so that the remaining students know whether to focus on land features or water features.

5. Have your students create their own fantasy islands, each incorporating at least ten land and water features. Encourage your students to be creative, but remind them that their features must make sense (e.g., the source of a river must come before any branches).

6. Discuss how their maps illustrate the answer to the central question on page 12.

Physical Map of Fantasy Island

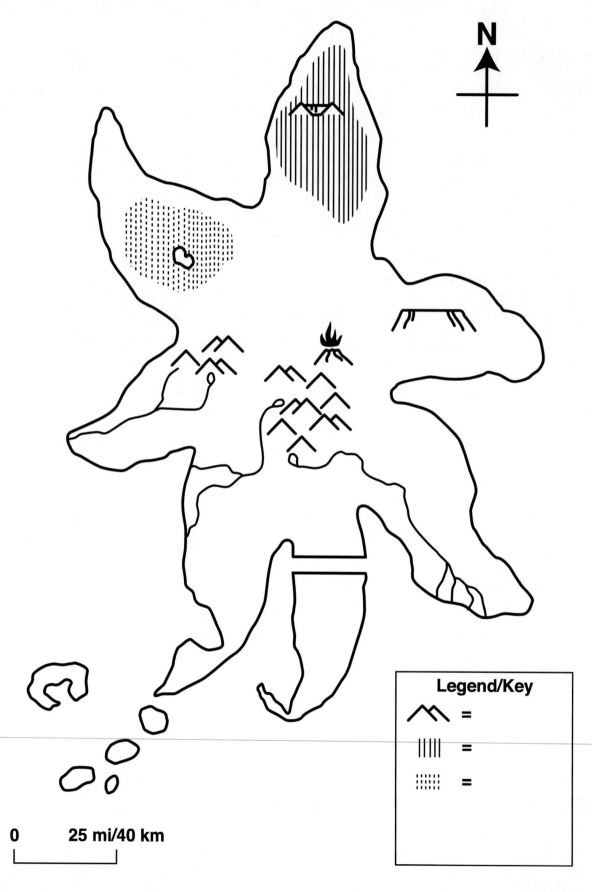

N

Legend/Key

⋀⋀ =

||||| =

⠿ =

0   25 mi/40 km

Feature Cards

archipelago	**source**	**mouth**
tributary	**mountain range**	**isthmus**
strait	**desert**	**oasis**
bay	**gulf**	**harbor**
canal	**tundra**	**glacier**
plateau	**volcano**	**delta**
peninsula	**cape**	**river**
atoll	**lagoon**	**branch**

Physical Map of Fantasy Island Key

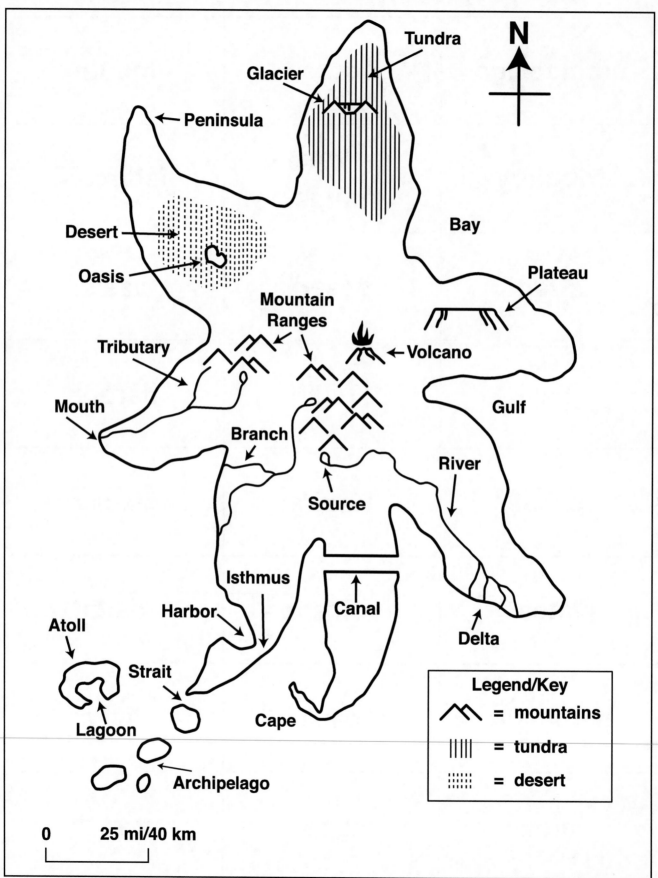

Which Way to the Pencil Sharpener?

Overview

In this lesson, students define map components and examine their uses. Students first examine a map of a known area, such as their school, making conclusions about map components. Then, students create maps on their own and use those maps to complete treasure hunts.

The answer key for student reproducibles is located at the end of the lesson. It is helpful for the teacher to examine such keys before beginning the lesson or distributing any reproducibles to the class. This type of advance inspection will (1) improve teacher understanding and presentation, (2) prepare the teacher for possible alternative student responses, (3) help with classroom time management, and (4) result in optimum focus and effectiveness for the activity.

Courtesy of www.clipart.com

Objective

- Students will understand the characteristics and uses of maps, globes, and other geographic tools and technologies.

Central Question

How do map components help people read maps?

Materials

You will need to prepare and/or provide the following:

- *Brainstorming Web* (1 per student), page 20
- overhead transparency of the floor plan of your school or other well-known building in your area (This map needs to show a title, compass rose, scale, and legend/key. If any of these map components are missing, add them.)

- *Map Component Notes* (1 per student), page 21
- *Treasure Hunt Incentives* (cut apart; 1 per student), page 22
- blank paper, 8" x 11" or larger (1 per student)
- rulers
- coloring materials

Answer Key

Map Components Key . . . . .page 23

Which Way to the Pencil Sharpener? *(cont.)*

Directions

Day One

1. Pass out copies of the *Brainstorming Web* to your students.

2. Begin by asking your students what makes a map useful. Have your students brainstorm alone, in pairs, or as a class. You will revisit their answers at the end of the activity. You may wish to have a student record the answers on the overhead.

3. Tell your students that they are going to learn how to use maps successfully and how to make maps that are easy to use.

4. Project the map of the school (or other building) on the overhead, and distribute copies of *Map Component Notes* to your students.

5. Direct a class discussion on map components (title, compass rose, scale, legend/key). Have your students complete the questions on *Map Component Notes* during your discussion.

Day Two

1. Briefly review yesterday's discussion and notes.

2. Distribute blank paper and rulers to your students and help them map the classroom individually. Let them know that they will use their maps (and only their maps) to complete a treasure hunt, so they need to work carefully and completely.

3. Give your students about 25 minutes to complete their maps. Each map should include a title, compass rose, scale, and legend or key.

4. Go back to the brainstorming results and, as a class, make three generalizations about what makes a map useful. In holding this discussion, make sure you guide students in answering the central question from page 17.

5. Allow your students to make adjustments to their maps, based on your generalizations.

6. You may want to collect the maps from your students so that everyone is prepared for the next day's activity.

Day Three

1. Before class, fill out and copy the *Treasure Hunt Incentives* for your students. See page 176 for *Incentive Suggestions*.

2. Distribute copies of the *Treasure Hunt Incentives* to your students. Place students into pairs. Have them record their partners' names on their copies of the sheet. Also give them their maps, if you collected them.

Which Way to the Pencil Sharpener? *(cont.)*

Directions *(cont.)*

Day Three *(cont.)*

3. Within each pair, students should assign each other a letter (*A* or *B*).

4. All the *A*-students should hide their incentives somewhere in the room while the *B*-students put their heads down. (No peeking!)

5. Students switch, with *A*'s putting their heads down and *B*'s hiding their incentives.

6. Once all the incentives are hidden, students write directions so their partners can find their incentives, using only the maps they created. Each set of directions should refer students to the scale, compass rose, and legend on the map.

7. Students switch directions and maps in pairs and use the maps to locate the incentives that their partners hid. Students should check their locations on the maps with their partners before looking for the incentives.

8. It may be helpful to your students for you to model this activity for them. Hide an incentive before they arrive, and create an overhead of your own map of the classroom. Give students directions orally or on paper to find the incentive you hid.

9. *Arts Integration:* Explain to your students that a collage is a series of overlapping pictures with a common theme, or meaning. Have your students create a collage that clearly represents each of the map components and their purpose, answering the central question "How do map components help us read maps?" To make their collages more polished, you might ask your students to create their collages in specific shapes (such as squares or maps of the United States) or to create borders for their collages. You may find it helpful to coordinate this activity with your school's art teacher.

Brainstorming Web

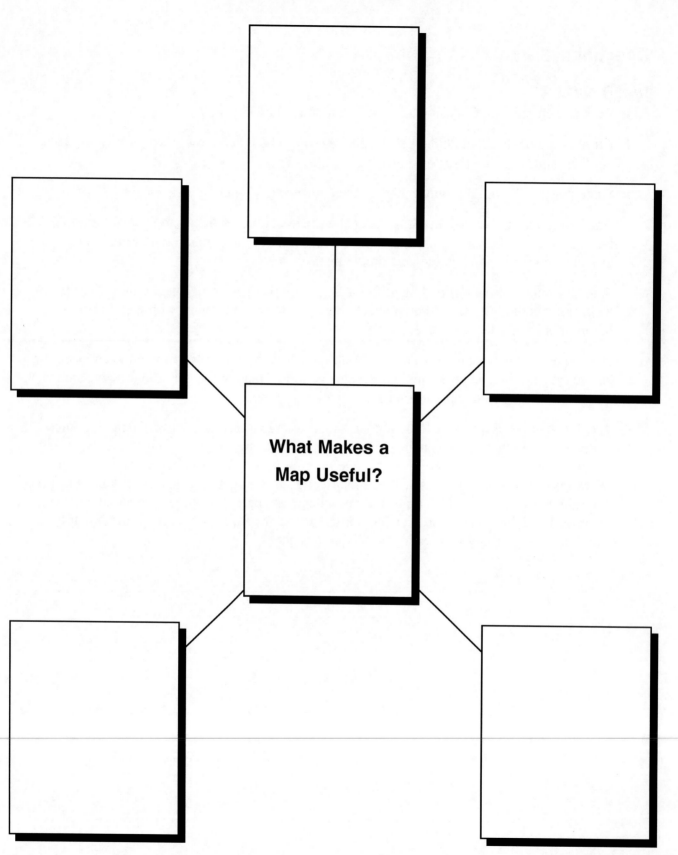

**What Makes a
Map Useful?**

Map Component Notes

Directions: Use the map on the overhead to answer the following questions.

1. What does this map show? _____

2. How would someone else know what this map shows? _____

   _____

3. What kind of information makes a map title useful? _____

   _____

4. What is in the northeast corner of the building? _____

   _____

5. How did you determine which is the northeast corner? _____

   _____

6. What is the purpose of a compass rose? _____

   _____

7. How wide is the building? _____

8. How do you know? _____

9. What is the purpose of a scale? _____

   _____

10. What is the difference on this map between the windows and the doors?

    _____

11. How would someone who had never been in this building know which
    symbols are windows and which are doors?

    _____

12. What is the purpose of the legend, or key?

    _____

Treasure Hunt Incentives

This certificate entitles _____

Student Name

to

_____

_____   _____
Signature   Date

This certificate entitles _____

Student Name

to

_____

_____   _____
Signature   Date

This certificate entitles _____

Student Name

to

_____

_____   _____
Signature   Date

Map Components Key

Directions: Use the map on the overhead to answer the following questions.

1. What does this map show? *Answers will vary depending on the map you used.*

2. How would someone else know what this map shows? *They could read the title of the map.*

3. What kind of information makes a map title useful? *Most map titles include the name of the area and what type of information is shown (physical, political, vegetation, etc.).*

4. What is in the northeast corner of the building? *Answers will vary.*

5. How did you determine which is the northeast corner? *by using the compass rose*

6. What is the purpose of a compass rose? *The compass rose gives cardinal (N, S, E, W) and intermediate (NE, SE, SW, NW) directions.*

7. How wide is the building? *Answers will vary.*

8. How do you know? *by using the scale*

9. What is the purpose of a scale? *The scale shows the size of the area and the objects within it. Everything on the map must be in the same scale.*

10. What is the difference on this map between the windows and the doors? *Answers will vary.*

11. How would someone who had never been in this building know which symbols are windows and which are doors? *by using the legend (or key)*

12. What is the purpose of the legend, or key? *The legend/key explains the meaning of all of the symbols, colors, and lines on the map.*

Perspective Detectives

Overview

In this activity, students take photographs of familiar objects in unfamiliar ways. Then, they analyze photographs taken by other students and examine several old maps to hypothesize about their purposes and perspectives. Finally, students create maps of their classroom using their unique photographs from the beginning of the activity.

The answer key for student reproducibles is located at the end of the lesson. It is helpful for the teacher to examine such keys before beginning the lesson or distributing any reproducibles to the class. This type of advance inspection will (1) improve teacher understanding and presentation, (2) prepare the teacher for possible alternative student responses, (3) help with classroom time management, and (4) result in optimum focus and effectiveness for the activity.

Courtesy of www.photos.com

Objective

- Students will understand the characteristics and uses of maps, globes, and other geographic tools and technologies.

Central Question

Why are there different types of maps?

Materials

You will need to prepare and/or provide the following:

- digital or disposable cameras (one per group)
- *Photo Sheet* (cut apart; one per group), page 27
- *What Is It?* (one per student), page 28
- *Global Perspective* (one per student), pages 29–30
- one set of *Global Images*, pages 31–36

- construction paper or other heavy paper
- scissors
- glue

Answer Key

Global Perspective Key . . . . .page 37

Perspective Detectives *(cont.)*

Directions

Day One (This activity may not take an entire period.)

1. Before class, you may wish to take a sample photograph of a common object from an uncommon angle to show your students (e.g., photograph a student desk from underneath). Ask your students to guess what your photograph shows.

2. Divide your class into groups of five or six students.

3. Give each group a digital or disposable camera. Have each student in the group take one photograph of a common object from an uncommon angle. In order to make the mapping activity at the end of the lesson easier, you may wish to divide your room into zones and assign each group a zone.

4. Ask students to record their names on the *Photo Sheet*. (This will help you to sort the photographs later and return them to their owners.)

5. Collect the cameras and the *Photo Sheets*. If you used disposable cameras, get the photographs developed before the next day. If you used a digital camera, print the photographs before the next day.

Day Two

1. Before class, arrange and number the photographs. Then, create a display for your students to examine. You can place them in any order you want.

2. When your students arrive, distribute copies of *What Is It?* to them. Have them examine the photographs from the day before. Tell them to record their guesses for each photo. When everyone has viewed all of the photos, have the owners claim them. (Use the *Photo Sheets* to help students pick the correct photos.)

3. Go over students' guesses and call on the owners of the photographs to reveal their objects. Discuss perspective with your students and the fact that Earth can be examined from different perspectives, using the following questions:

   - What is *perspective*?
   - Why do people have different perspectives?
   - How might perspective relate to maps?

Day Three

1. Before class, display the various *Global Images* sheets in stations around the room. You may wish to incorporate other types of maps as well, such as cartograms, Peters projections, and southern-perspective maps.

2. Arrange your students into groups of three or four and distribute copies of the *Global Perspective* sheets to the students.

Perspective Detectives *(cont.)*

Directions *(cont.)*

Day Three *(cont.)*

3. Give your students about 20 minutes to go through the *Global Image* stations in their groups. As they move around the room, they should answer the *Global Perspective* questions.

4. Have the students return to their seats and, as a class, review their answers.

5. *Arts Integration:* In the following steps, students will create photographic maps of the classroom using their images from the opening activity.

6. Put students back in their original photograph groups. Each group should create a map of the classroom (or of their zone, if you divided the room into zones).

7. They should paste the photographs onto a single piece of construction paper (or other thick paper). Students may trim their photographs so that they fit together better. If you used zones, create a single classroom map by challenging your students to connect the zones correctly.

Extension Idea

- You may wish to offer your students the opportunity to create a map of the world, using continents from different types of maps. For example, a single map might contain a Peters projection of North America, a satellite photo of South America, a cartogram of Europe, a Mercator projection of Africa, and so on.

Photo Sheet

Group number: _____   Class period: _____

Camera # _____

Photo #1 taken by _____   Photo #2 taken by _____

Photo #3 taken by _____   Photo #4 taken by _____

Photo #5 taken by _____   Photo #6 taken by _____

- -

Group number: _____   Class period: _____

Camera # _____

Photo #1 taken by _____   Photo #2 taken by _____

Photo #3 taken by _____   Photo #4 taken by _____

Photo #5 taken by _____   Photo #6 taken by _____

- -

Group number: _____   Class period: _____

Camera # _____

Photo #1 taken by _____   Photo #2 taken by _____

Photo #3 taken by _____   Photo #4 taken by _____

Photo #5 taken by _____   Photo #6 taken by _____

- -

Group number: _____   Class period: _____

Camera # _____

Photo #1 taken by _____   Photo #2 taken by _____

Photo #3 taken by _____   Photo #4 taken by _____

Photo #5 taken by _____   Photo #6 taken by _____

What Is It?

Examine the photographs taken by your classmates. What do you think they were capturing? Write your guesses in the spaces below.

1. _____
2. _____
3. _____
4. _____
5. _____
6. _____
7. _____
8. _____
9. _____
10. _____
11. _____
12. _____
13. _____
14. _____
15. _____
16. _____
17. _____
18. _____
19. _____
20. _____
21. _____
22. _____
23. _____
24. _____

Global Perspective

Global Image 1

What part of Earth does this image show? _____

Whose perspective does this image show? _____

What might be the purpose of this image? _____

_____

What are the advantages of this image? _____

_____

_____

Global Image 2

What part of Earth does this image show? _____

Whose perspective does this image show? _____

What might be the purpose of this image? _____

_____

What are the advantages of this image? _____

_____

_____

Global Image 3

What part of Earth does this image show? _____

Whose perspective does this image show? _____

What might be the purpose of this image? _____

_____

What are the advantages of this image? _____

_____

Global Perspective *(cont.)*

Global Image 4

What part of Earth does this image show? _____

Whose perspective does this image show? _____

What might be the purpose of this image? _____

_____

What are the advantages of this image? _____

_____

_____

Global Image 5

What part of Earth does this image show? _____

Whose perspective does this image show? _____

What might be the purpose of this image? _____

_____

What are the advantages of this image? _____

_____

_____

Global Image 6

What part of Earth does this image show? _____

Whose perspective does this image show? _____

What might be the purpose of this image? _____

_____

What are the advantages of this image? _____

_____

_____

Global Image 1

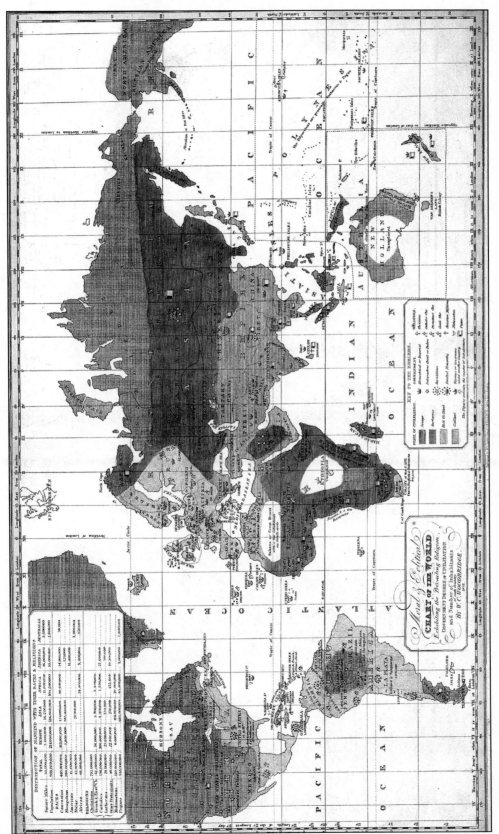

Courtesy of www.photos.com

Global Image 2

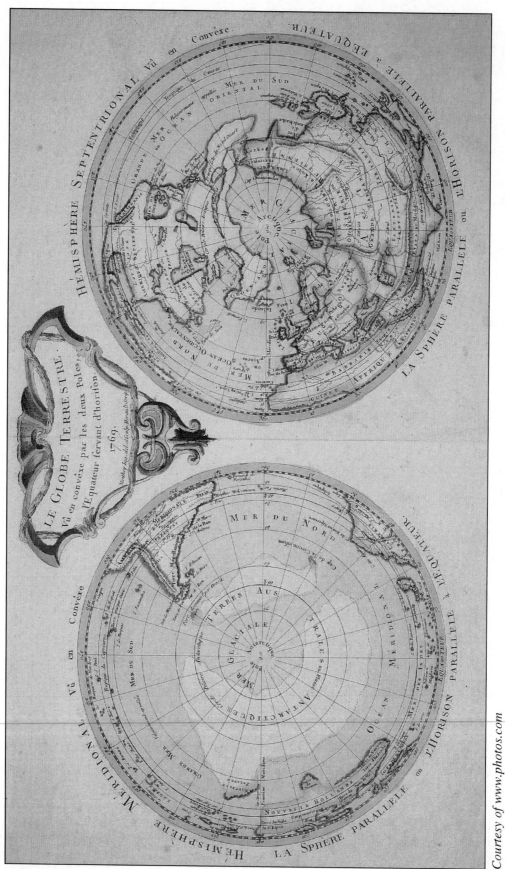

Global Image 3

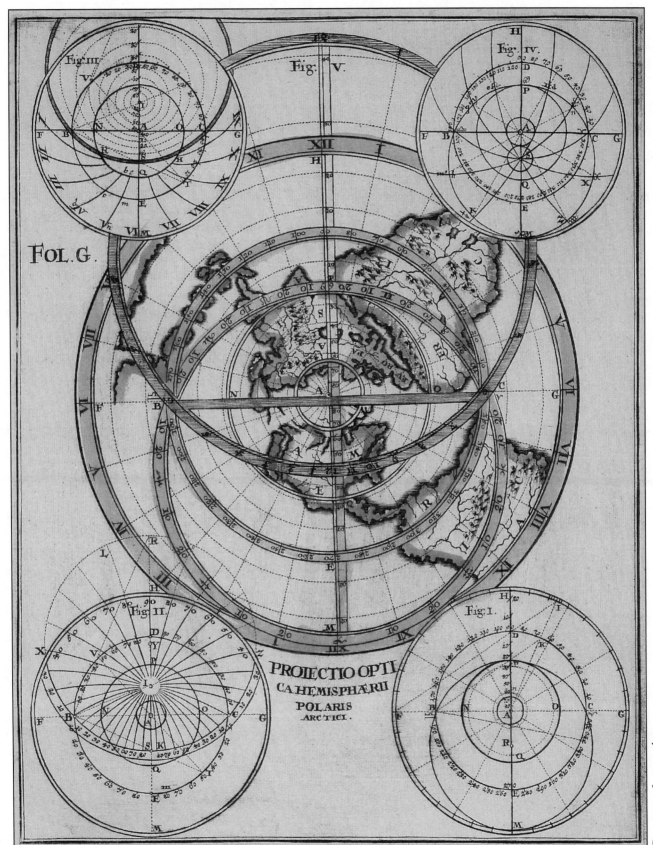

Global Image 4

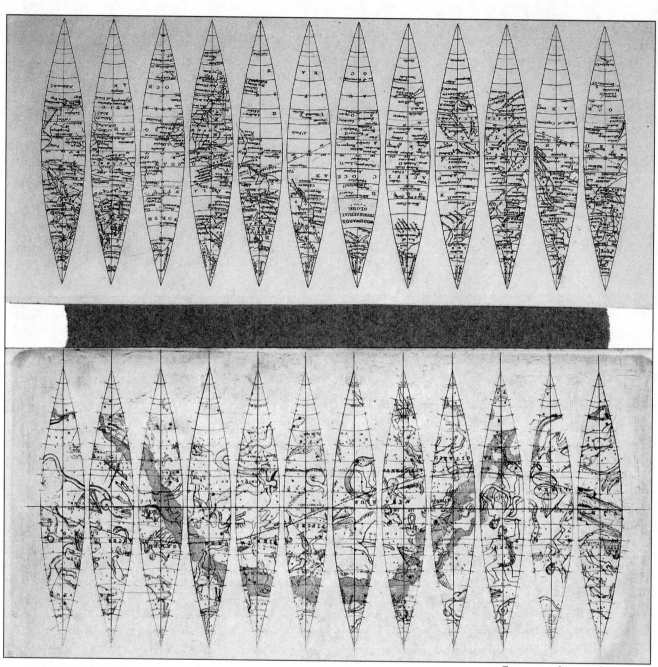

Courtesy of www.photos.com

Global Image 5

Courtesy of www.photos.com

Global Image 6

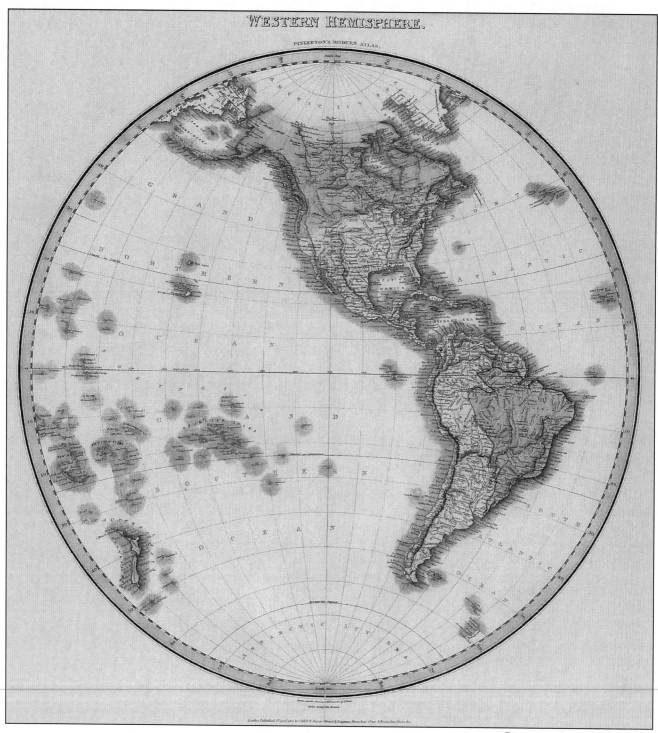

Courtesy of www.photos.com

Global Perspective Key

While your students' answers may vary, some basic answers are included here, along with a little background on each image.

Global Image 1 (Mercator Projection)

What part of Earth does this image show? *the whole world*

Whose perspective does this image show? *Europeans (Europe is in the center.)*

What might be the purpose of this image? *Sailors might use it for navigation.*

What are the advantages of this image? *Orientation is easy to see.*

Global Image 2 (1769 French Polar Map)

What part of Earth does this image show? *the North and South Poles*

Whose perspective does this image show? *people living in extreme north or south*

What might be the purpose of this image? *exploration of northern and southern areas*

What are the advantages of this image? *easy to see relationship between ends of continents; Great Circle Route for planes*

Global Image 3 (North Pole Map, 1700)

What part of Earth does this image show? *the North Pole*

Whose perspective does this image show? *northern hemisphere*

What might be the purpose of this image? *showing relationships between continents (interconnecting circles)*

What are the advantages of this image? *shows the relationship between continents at the North Pole*

Global Image 4 (Global Gores, 1860)

What part of Earth does this image show? *the whole world*

Whose perspective does this image show? *cartographer; someone concerned with accuracy in maps*

What might be the purpose of this image? *to show true direction, distance, and size*

What are the advantages of this image? *very accurate (but very hard to read)*

Global Image 5 (Aerial Photograph)

What part of Earth does this image show? *an urban area*

Whose perspective does this image show? *a pilot*

What might be the purpose of this image? *tracking urban development; spying; mapping local roads*

What are the advantages of this image? *gives great detail of a small area of Earth*

Global Image 6 (Hemispheric Map, 1812)

What part of Earth does this image show? *the western hemisphere*

Whose perspective does this image show? *Americans (north and south)*

What might be the purpose of this image? *travel within the western hemisphere*

What are the advantages of this image? *Smaller area allows cartographer to show more detail.*

Grid and Bear It!

Overview

In this activity, students learn to use latitude and longitude to identify absolute location. Students will read a brief introduction, diagram and act out latitude and longitude, play a version of the old game *Battleship* to reinforce their knowledge, and create books to help them remember the process of finding latitude and longitude.

Courtesy of www.clipart.com

The answer key for student reproducibles is located at the end of the lesson. It is helpful for the teacher to examine such keys before beginning the lesson or distributing any reproducibles to the class. This type of advance inspection will (1) improve teacher understanding and presentation, (2) prepare the teacher for possible alternative student responses, (3) help with classroom time management, and (4) result in optimum focus and effectiveness for the activity.

Objectives

- Students will understand the characteristics and uses of maps, globes, and other geographic tools and technologies.
- Students will understand the characteristics and uses of spatial organization of Earth's surface.

Central Question

How are latitude and longitude used to locate places on the earth?

Materials

You will need to prepare and/or provide the following:

- class set of *Introduction to Latitude and Longitude*, page 40
- overhead transparencies of *Latitude and Longitude Notes*, page 41–42
- *Battleship Grid* (one per student), page 43
- *Directions for Creating an Eight-Page*

- *Book* (one or more copies), page 44
- *Book Template* (cut apart; one per student), page 45
- construction paper
- scissors; crayons, markers, etc.

Answer Keys

Latitude and Longitude Notes: Latitude Key . . . . .page 46
Latitude and Longitude Notes: Longitude Key . . . . .page 47

Grid and Bear It! *(cont.)*

Directions

Day One

1. Distribute *Introduction to Latitude and Longitude* and read it as a class.

2. Lead the class through *Latitude and Longitude Notes*, diagramming first latitude and then longitude. Use the answer keys on pages 46–47 to guide your model diagrams.

3. Arrange desks in a grid pattern. Assign each student an absolute location.

4. Call out an absolute location and have the corresponding student stand. To make this part easier for your students, you may wish to use numbers for the rows and letters for the columns for the first round. Once they understand the activity, you can use numbers for both rows and columns.

5. Next, assign cardinal directions (north, south, east, and west) to the walls of your room and repeat the game. This works best with an odd number of rows and columns so that you can have a row for the equator and a column for the prime meridian.

Day Two

1. Pass out copies of the *Battleship Grid*. Have students label the equator and the prime meridian. Then, they should label the lines of latitude and longitude.

2. Students should place five "ships" (of the following lengths: 2 squares, 3 squares, 3 squares, 4 squares, and 5 squares) somewhere on their *Battleship Grids*. They can use *X*'s, *O*'s, or simple drawings. You may wish to have students place one ship in each quadrant of the grid, while the fifth ship can be anywhere.

3. In pairs, students try to guess the locations of each others' ships by calling out coordinates. You may wish to have students give each other hints, such as "warm" or "cold."

4. Students take turns, and the first person to sink all five ships wins.

5. *Arts Integration:* Your students will create step-by-step books for them to use as references throughout their work with latitude and longitude.

6. Give each of your students a piece of construction paper.

7. Lead your students through the *Directions for Creating an Eight-Page Book*. You may wish to make additional copies of these directions to give to your students.

8. Pass out the *Book Template*, scissors, and crayons or markers to your students.

9. Allow your students to cut out the strips and arrange them in the correct order. Check your students' work before they glue the steps into their books.

10. Give your students ample time to assemble their books and create an illustration for each page.

Introduction to Latitude and Longitude

What kinds of grids do you use in your everyday life? In your math and science classes, you may have learned how to use and create graphs. If you play team sports like soccer or basketball, you may know about zones, which are similar to grids. How many of you have ever played tic-tac-toe? Grids are used to define a space, giving a limit in four directions: up, down, left, and right.

The global grid allows us to determine the absolute location of a place on Earth. Instead of using the words *up*, *down*, *left*, and *right*, we use *north*, *south*, *east*, and *west*.

The north and south boundaries are created by lines of latitude. **Latitude** measures how far a place is from the equator. The equator is measured as 0°. It is neither north nor south, because it is in the middle. Lines of latitude are called *parallels* because they are parallel to each other and never meet. The farthest away a place can be from the equator is the North or South Pole. The poles are 90° away from the equator, so the highest latitude you can have is 90° north or 90° south. Latitude numbers are usually found on the sides of most maps. Climate is heavily related to latitude. Generally, the farther away you are from the equator (north or south), the colder the climate is.

The east and west boundaries are created by lines of longitude. **Longitude** measures the distance a place is east or west of the prime meridian. The prime meridian is measured as 0°. Like the equator, it is in the middle, so it is neither east nor west. Longitude lines are called *meridians*, and they meet at the North and South Poles, like the sections of an orange. The largest measure of longitude is 180° (roughly, the International Date Line), halfway around the globe. Longitude numbers are generally found on the tops of most maps. Time zones correspond to longitude.

These two sets of lines work together to form the global grid. With latitude and longitude you can determine the exact, or absolute, location of a place. Latitude always comes first and longitude second. The absolute location of a place (its latitude and longitude) is called a *coordinate*. Remember to always include the cardinal direction (north, south, east, and west) after the numbers in the coordinate.

Latitude and Longitude Notes

Latitude

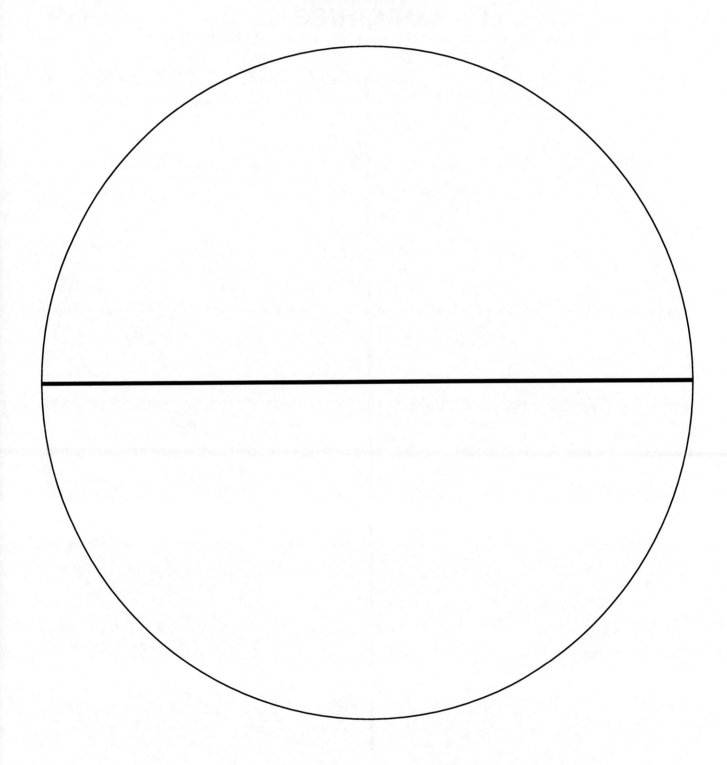

Latitude and Longitude Notes *(cont.)*

Longitude

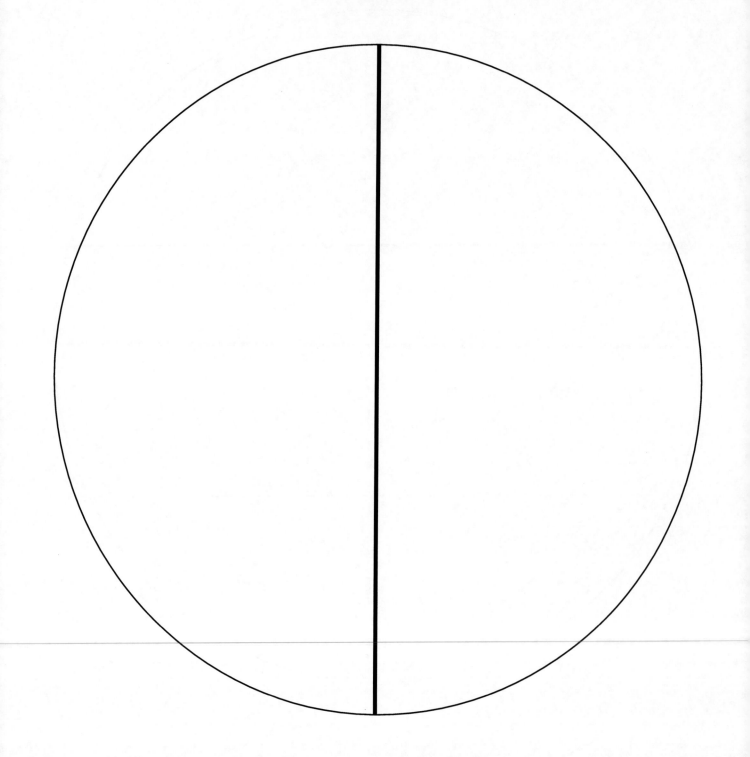

Battleship Grid

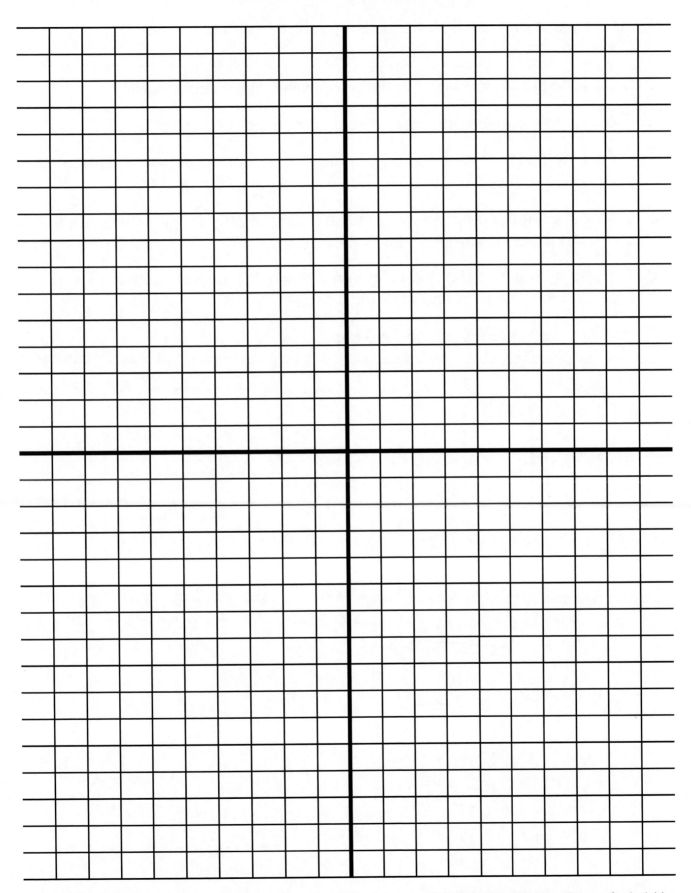

Directions for Creating an Eight-Page Book

1. Fold a piece of 9" x 12" construction paper in half lengthwise ("hot dog" fold).

2. Unfold the paper and fold it in half widthwise ("hamburger" fold).

3. Fold it in half again lengthwise, without unfolding the last fold.

4. Unfold the last fold, and use scissors to cut along the center line on the closed side of the fold, but only halfway through to the next fold.

5. Unfold the paper completely. Fold it in half along the first lengthwise fold and push the ends towards each other.

6. The paper should fold naturally in one direction. Smooth out the creases and fold the remaining end under the back.

7. Now you have an eight-page mini-book.

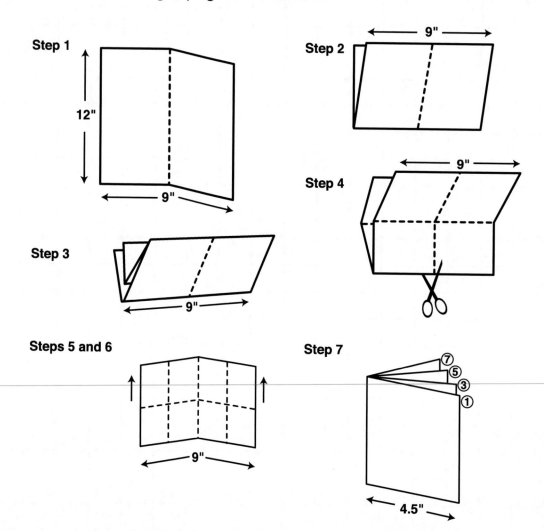

Book Template

Directions: Cut out the following strips and glue them into your book in the correct order. You may wish to have your teacher check the order before you glue. Add an illustration to each page to help you remember the steps.

• Find the numbers on the side of the map.
• Find the numbers at the top or bottom of the map.
• Is your location north or south of the equator?
• How many degrees away from the prime meridian is it?
• Find the prime meridian.
• Is your location east or west of the prime meridian?
• How many degrees away from the equator is it?
• Find the equator.

Directions: Cut out the following strips and glue them into your book in the correct order. You may wish to have your teacher check the order before you glue. Add an illustration to each page to help you remember the steps.

• Find the numbers on the side of the map.
• Find the numbers at the top or bottom of the map.
• Is your location north or south of the equator?
• How many degrees away from the prime meridian is it?
• Find the prime meridian.
• Is your location east or west of the prime meridian?
• How many degrees away from the equator is it?
• Find the equator.

Latitude and Longitude Notes: Latitude Key

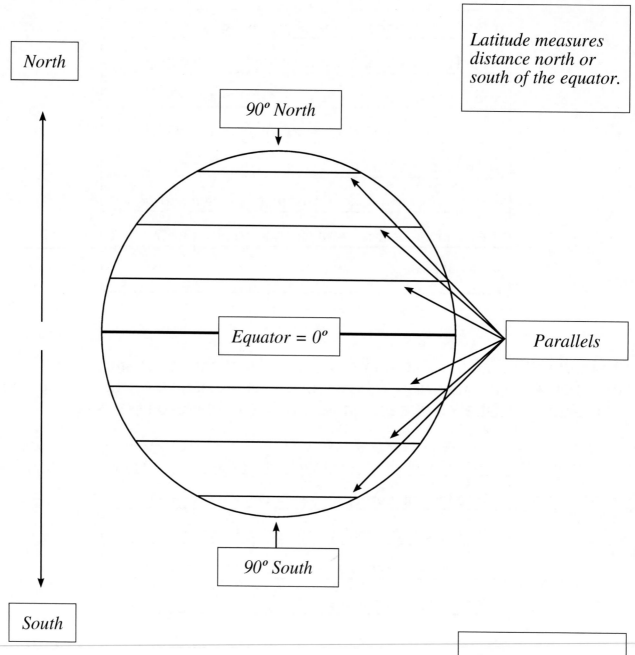

North

90° North

Latitude measures distance north or south of the equator.

Equator = 0°

Parallels

90° South

South

The higher the latitude number, the farther away it is from the equator. 90° is the farthest.

Latitude and Longitude Notes: Longitude Key

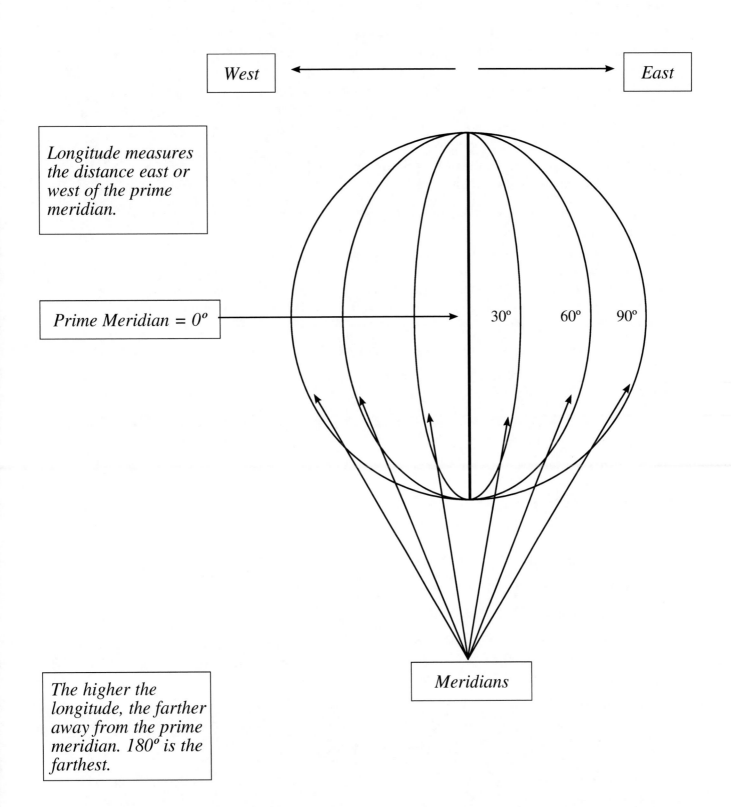

West ← → East

Longitude measures the distance east or west of the prime meridian.

Prime Meridian = 0°

30°   60°   90°

Meridians

The higher the longitude, the farther away from the prime meridian. 180° is the farthest.

Read, Read, Read Your Map

Overview

Because understanding and using latitude and longitude can be difficult skills for students to master, you may wish to give your students additional practice. In this activity, students reinforce their knowledge of latitude and longitude. They review the process of finding the latitude and longitude of a location by working in pairs, practice finding latitude and longitude by "hunting" for their teacher, and strengthen their knowledge by creating songs about latitude and longitude.

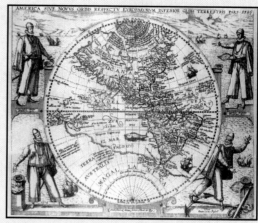

Courtesy of The Library of Congress

The answer key for student reproducibles is located at the end of the lesson. It is helpful for the teacher to examine such keys before beginning the lesson or distributing any reproducibles to the class. This type of advance inspection will (1) improve teacher understanding and presentation, (2) prepare the teacher for possible alternative student responses, (3) help with classroom time management, and (4) result in optimum focus and effectiveness for the activity.

Objective

- Students will understand the characteristics and uses of maps, globes, and other geographic tools and technologies.

Central Question

How are latitude and longitude used to locate places on Earth?

Materials

You will need to prepare and/or provide the following:

- *Latitude and Longitude Practice Sheet* (one per pair), page 50
- *Teacher Hunt #1* (one per student), page 51
- *Teacher Hunt #2* (one per student), page 52

- class set of *Latitude and Longitude Song*, page 53 (cut apart)
- atlases and/or other reference maps
- rhythm instruments (optional)

Answer Keys

Read, Read, Read Your Map *(cont.)*

Directions

Day One

1. Before class, make half as many copies of the *Latitude and Longitude Practice Sheet* as you have students. Cut each sheet in half vertically, following the dotted line. You may wish to put a different symbol along the dotted line of each sheet. When you cut the sheets apart, your students can use the symbols to find their partners.

2. If your students created latitude and longitude books in the previous lesson, ask your students to trade books. They will use one another's books for reference as they work.

3. Pass out copies of the *Latitude and Longitude Practice Sheet*, and arrange your students in pairs. Or, have them use the symbols to find their partners.

4. Give each pair an atlas or other map reference.

5. Pairs should take turns quizzing each other on the locations on their sheets. Tell your students to alternate between giving their partners the names of the cities and the latitudes and longitudes.

Day Two

1. You'll work on the *Teacher Hunt* today. There are two different versions included. You may wish to use both versions, or you may wish to save version two for later practice. Distribute whichever version(s) you are using.

2. Working alone or in pairs, students solve the mystery of their teacher's location.

3. Go over the *Teacher Hunt* exercise as a class. You may wish to have students create their own Teacher Hunts (or Student Hunts).

4. *Arts Integration:* Pass out rhythm instruments if you have them. Lead the class in singing the *Latitude and Longitude Song* to the tune of "Row, Row, Row Your Boat." After one or two rehearsals, you may wish to have students sing the song in rounds.

5. Students should write their own songs answering the central question, "How are latitude and longitude used to locate places on Earth's surface?" You might suggest that students use a nursery rhyme, a rap, or a commercial jingle using a simple melody. You may find it helpful to coordinate this activity with your school's music teacher.

Latitude and Longitude Practice Sheet

Quiz your partner on the locations below. You may give your partner either the latitude and longitude or the city and country.

1. 51°N   0°
2. 30°N   31°E
3. 12°S   77°W
4. 33°S   151°E
5. 35°N   139°E
6. 37°N   122°W
7. 41°N   29°E
8. 50°N   30°E
9. 26°S   28°E
10. 33°N   73°E

1. London, England
2. Cairo, Egypt
3. Lima, Peru
4. Sydney, Australia
5. Tokyo, Japan
6. San Francisco, United States
7. Istanbul, Turkey
8. Kiev, Ukraine
9. Johannesburg, South Africa
10. Islamabad, Pakistan

Quiz your partner on the locations below. You may give your partner either the latitude and longitude or the city and country.

1. 33°N   44°E
2. 1°S   36°E
3. 41°S   174°E
4. 22°S   43°W
5. 55°N   37°E
6. 39°N   116°E
7. 28°N   77°E
8. 41°N   12°E
9. 37°N   23°E
10. 43°N   79°W

1. Baghdad, Iraq
2. Nairobi, Kenya
3. Wellington, New Zealand
4. Rio de Janeiro, Brazil
5. Moscow, Russia
6. Beijing, China
7. New Delhi, India
8. Rome, Italy
9. Athens, Greece
10. Toronto, Canada

Teacher Hunt #1

Oh no! Your teacher, _____, is missing! It's up to you to use your abundant geography skills to come to the rescue.

He/she was last seen at 22°S 17°E, in the city of _____ where he/she caught a ride on a camel because he/she was about to enter the _____ _____ Desert. From there, you find that he/she traveled west to reach the _____ Ocean.

You almost caught up with him/her at 22°S 43°W, where he/she got lost in the carnival crowd in _____. You pick up his/her trail again outside Punta Arenas (latitude: _____, longitude: _____), which is _____ of Rio. It's a good thing he/she dressed warmly because he/she is heading straight for Antarctica!

By the time you reach Antarctica, he/she is gone again, this time heading _____ ___ to Australia. You just miss him/her in Perth, a city located at latitude: _____, longitude: ____. He/she traveled from there by boat along the _____ Ocean to the world's largest continent, _____. He/she got off the boat in Chennai (Madras), located at latitude: ____, longitude: _____. Once in Chennai, he/she flew to a city located at 43°N 131°E, which is _____ _____. From there, he/she boarded a train and rode the world's longest railroad, from Vladivostok to Moscow (latitude: ____, longitude: ____).

Once there, he/she caught a ride to a port city located at 60°N 24°E, which is _____. He/she took a short ferry ride to the major city across the Baltic Sea, _____, located at latitude: ____, longitude: _____. There, he/she boarded a plane and returned to the major city near your school, _____ _____, whose latitude and longitude are _____. You meet up with him/her at baggage claim and drive him/her back to school, located at latitude: ____ and longitude: _____.

Teacher Hunt #2

Oh no! Your teacher, _____, is missing! It's up to you to use your abundant geography skills to come to the rescue.

He/she was last seen at 27°N 85°E in the city of _____, where he/she put on hiking boots and a warm coat, because he/she was about to enter the _____ Mountains. From there, you find that he/she traveled east to reach the _____ Ocean.

You almost caught up with him/her at 33°S 151°E, where he/she got lost in the famous opera house in _____. You pick up his/her trail again near the Panama Canal, which is _____ of South America. It's a good thing he/she dressed for warm weather, because he/she is heading straight for the beach!

By the time you reach the beach, he/she is gone again, this time heading _____ to Morocco. You just miss him/her in Rabat, a city located at latitude: _____, longitude: _____. He/she traveled from there by boat across the _____ Sea to the continent made up almost entirely of peninsulas, _____. He/she got off the boat in the city located at 38°N 9°W called _____. Once there, he/she flew to a city located at 43°N 131°E, _____. From there, he/she boarded a train and rode the world's longest railroad, from Vladivostok to Moscow (latitude: _____, longitude: _____).

Once there, he/she caught a ride to a port city located at 59°N 24°E (_____). He/she took a short ferry ride to the major city across the Gulf of Finland, _____, located at latitude: _____, longitude: _____. There, he/she boarded a plane and returned to the major city near your school, _____, whose latitude and longitude are _____. You meet up with him/her at baggage claim and drive him/her back to school, located at latitude: _____ and longitude: _____.

Latitude and Longitude Song

Latitude and Longitude Song

(Sung to the tune of "Row, Row, Row your Boat")

Lat . . . lat . . . latitude

How far north or south?

Side of the, side of the, side of the map

The equator starts the route.

Long . . . long . . . longitude

How far east or west?

Top of the, top of the, top of the map

Meridians tell the rest.

Latitude and longitude

It's just a simple fact.

These are what you have to use

When location is exact.

Latitude and Longitude Song

(Sung to the tune of "Row, Row, Row your Boat")

Lat . . . lat . . . latitude

How far north or south?

Side of the, side of the, side of the map

The equator starts the route.

Long . . . long . . . longitude

How far east or west?

Top of the, top of the, top of the map

Meridians tell the rest.

Latitude and longitude

It's just a simple fact.

These are what you have to use

When location is exact.

Latitude and Longitude Song

(Sung to the tune of "Row, Row, Row your Boat")

Lat . . . lat . . . latitude

How far north or south?

Side of the, side of the, side of the map

The equator starts the route.

Long . . . long . . . longitude

How far east or west?

Top of the, top of the, top of the map

Meridians tell the rest.

Latitude and longitude

It's just a simple fact.

These are what you have to use

When location is exact.

Latitude and Longitude Song

(Sung to the tune of "Row, Row, Row your Boat")

Lat . . . lat . . . latitude

How far north or south?

Side of the, side of the, side of the map

The equator starts the route.

Long . . . long . . . longitude

How far east or west?

Top of the, top of the, top of the map

Meridians tell the rest.

Latitude and longitude

It's just a simple fact.

These are what you have to use

When location is exact.

Teacher Hunt #1 Key

Oh no! Your teacher, _____, is missing! It's up to you to use your abundant geography skills to come to the rescue.

He/she was last seen at 22°S 17°E, in the city of (*Windhoek*) where he/she caught a ride on a camel because he/she was about to enter the (*Namib*) Desert. From there, you find that he/she traveled west to reach the (*Atlantic*) Ocean.

You almost caught up with him/her at 22°S 43°W, where he/she got lost in the carnival crowd in (*Rio de Janeiro*). You pick up his/her trail again outside Punta Arenas (*53°S 70°W*) which is (*south*) of Rio. It's a good thing he/she dressed warmly because he/she is heading straight for Antarctica!

By the time you reach Antarctica, he/she is gone again, this time heading (*north*) to Australia. You just miss him/her in Perth, a city located at (*32°S 115°E*). He/she traveled from there by boat along the (*Indian*) Ocean to the world's largest continent, (*Asia*). He/she got off the boat in Chennai (Madras), located at (*13°N 80°E*). Once in Chennai, he/she flew to a city located at 43°N 131°E, which is (*Vladivostok*). From there, he/she boarded a train and rode the world's longest railroad, from Vladivostok to Moscow (*55°N 37°E*).

Once there, he/she caught a ride to a port city located at 60°N 24°E (*Helsinki*). He/she took a short ferry ride to the major city across the Baltic Sea, which is (*Stockholm*), located at (*59°N 18°E*). There, he/she boarded a plane and returned to the major city near your school, (*answer will vary*), whose latitude and longitude are (*answer will vary*). You meet up with him/her at baggage claim, and drive him/her back to school, located at (*answer will vary*).

Teacher Hunt #2 Key

Oh no! Your teacher, _____, is missing! It's up to you to use your abundant geography skills to come to the rescue.

He/she was last seen at 27°N 85°E in the city of (*Kathmandu*), where he/she put on hiking boots and a warm coat, because he/she was about to enter the (*Himalaya*) Mountains. From there, you find that he/she traveled east to reach the (*Pacific*) Ocean.

You almost caught up with him/her at 33°S 151°E, where he/she got lost in the famous opera house in (*Sydney*). You pick up his/her trail again near the Panama Canal, which is (*north*) of South America. It's a good thing he/she dressed for warm weather, because he/she is heading straight for the beach!

By the time you reach the beach, he/she is gone again, this time heading (*east*) to Morocco. You just miss him/her in Rabat, a city located at (*34°N 6°W*). He/she traveled from there by boat across the (*Mediterranean*) Sea to the continent made up almost entirely of peninsulas, (*Europe*). He/she got off the boat in the city located at 38°N 9°W called (*Lisbon*). Once there, he/she flew to a city located at 43°N 131°E, (*Vladivostok*). From there, he/she boarded a train and rode the world's longest railroad, from Vladivostok to Moscow (*55°N 37°E*).

Once there, he/she caught a ride to a port city located at 59°N 24°E (*Tallinn*). He/she took a short ferry ride to the major city across the Gulf of Finland, (*Helsinki*), located at (*60°N 24°E*). There, he/she boarded a plane and returned to the major city near your school, (*answer will vary*), whose latitude and longitude are (*answer will vary*). You meet up with him/her at baggage claim and drive him/her back to school, located at (*answer will vary*).

Weather or Not

Overview

In this lesson students learn the factors that determine an area's climate and how to read a climate graph. They use this knowledge to identify major cities based on their climates, and create tableaux to demonstrate major climate patterns and how they relate to location.

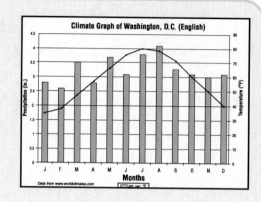

The answer key for student reproducibles is located at the end of the lesson. It is helpful for the teacher to examine such keys before beginning the lesson or distributing any reproducibles to the class. This type of advance inspection will (1) improve teacher understanding and presentation, (2) prepare the teacher for possible alternative student responses, (3) help with classroom time management, and (4) result in optimum focus and effectiveness for the activity.

Objective

- Students will understand the characteristics of ecosystems on Earth's surface.

Central Question

How is climate related to location?

Materials

You will need to prepare and/or provide the following:

- *Climate Notes* (one per student), page 58
- overhead transparency of *Climate Notes*
- overhead transparency or handouts of *Climate Graph for Washington, D.C.*, page 59
- *Climate Graphs* (Metric or English) (one per student), pages 60–63

- *World Climate Regions* (one per student), page 64
- Class set of *Climate Region Cards*, page 65
- Research resources for climate regions (e.g., Internet, atlas, textbooks)

Answer Keys

Weather or Not *(cont.)*

Directions

Day One

1. Distribute a copy of *Climate Notes* to each student, and put a copy on the overhead projector.

2. Lead a class discussion on climate, filling in the notes on the overhead as you go. Use page 66 as a reference as you work. Answer any student questions to make sure that students understand their notes.

3. Display on the overhead or pass out copies of *Climate Graph for Washington, D.C.* Explain that a climate graph shows both temperature and precipitation (the elements of climate) on one graph. Precipitation is shown by the bar graph and uses the left *y*-axis, while temperature is shown by the line graph and uses the right *y*-axis.

4. Distribute *Climate Graphs*, either the metric or the English version. Have students work in pairs to make observations about each graph, such as whether there are distinct seasons, which months are hottest, and if there is a rainy season. Then, ask students to assign a location to each climate graph based on their observations. (You may wish to provide a location word bank.) Go over the answers with your students.

5. For homework, have your students fill in the *World Climate Regions*. It may be helpful to assign textbook pages for reference.

Day Two

1. Go over the homework with your students.

2. *Arts Integration:* Arrange your students into groups of four or five.

3. Each group receives one *Climate Region Card*, and should then research its climate region's characteristics and location.

4. Explain to the class that they will create tableaux of their climate regions. A tableau is a "freeze frame" where students get into position and remain still. Explain that this is a technique used in theater to fully examine a moment. Actors freeze in position; then the director asks them questions about their character—how they feel at the moment, what they see, etc. The actors must answer in character. You may wish to have your students answer questions or have them simply freeze. Their tableaux must fully represent the relationship between climate and location. They may use basic props found around the room, but their main tool is their bodies.

5. The class guesses the climate region of each tableau.

6. You may wish to videotape or photograph each of the tableaux. You could create "climate stations" with the photos, where students can identify the climate region, choose one photo that they think best represents the climate, and explain why. Use the videos with other classes when time is more constrained.

7. Lead a class discussion on the connections between climate and location. Answer the central question from page 56. You can also use the following questions:

   • What characteristics do climates in low latitudes share? Middle latitudes? High latitudes?

   • Are there any climates that can be found in all three regions?

Climate Notes

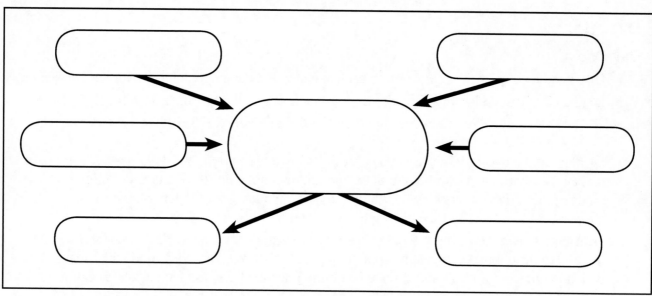

Climate is an area's _____. It consists of _____ and

_____ (rain, snow, etc.). There are four factors that affect climate. They are

_____, _____, _____,

and _____.

Latitude (distance from the _____)
- Climate gets _____ the farther you get from the _____.
- It doesn't matter whether you move _____ or _____.

Altitude (_____ above sea level)
- Higher altitude = _____, _____ climate
- Lower altitude = _____, _____ climate

Wind and Mountains
- Winds

  From _____ to _____ = "wet" winds. _____ will fall as air cools.

  From land to ocean = _____ _____
- Mountains

  As wind climbs a mountain, it _____ and causes _____. This is the ____

  _____ side of the mountain.

  Wind that makes it over the top is _____. This is the _____ side of the

  mountain.

Ocean Currents
- Currents can move _____ or _____ water from one part of the world to another.
- Water warms or cools the _____ above it.
- _____ cools and warms slower than _____.
- Ocean currents generally make a climate _____.

Climate Graph for Washington, D.C.

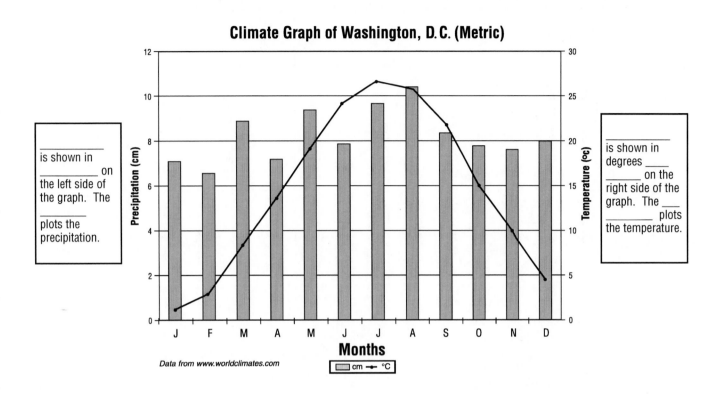

_____ is shown in _____ on the left side of the graph. The _____ plots the precipitation.

_____ is shown in degrees ____ _____ on the right side of the graph. The ___ _____ plots the temperature.

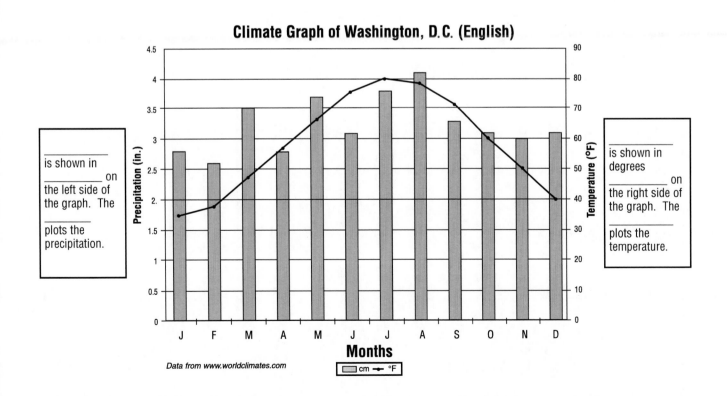

_____ is shown in _____ on the left side of the graph. The _____ plots the precipitation.

_____ is shown in degrees _____ on the right side of the graph. The _____ plots the temperature.

Climate Graphs *(Metric)*

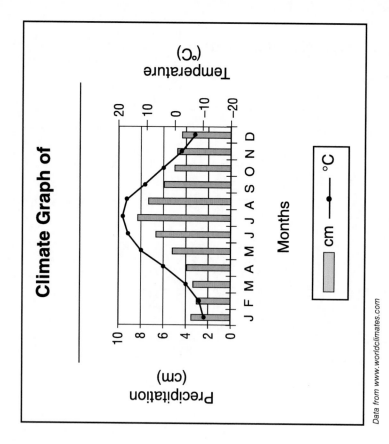

Data from www.worldclimates.com

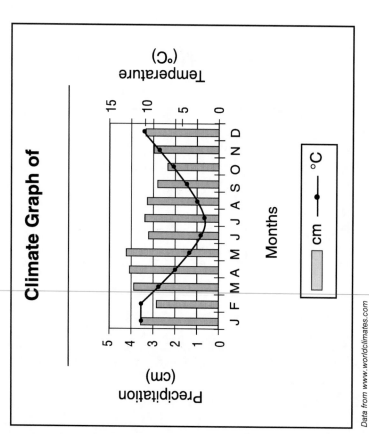

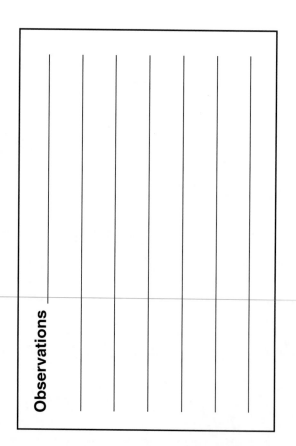

Data from www.worldclimates.com

Climate Graphs *(Metric)* *(cont.)*

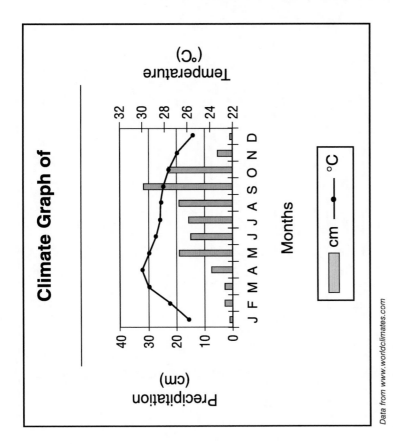

Observations

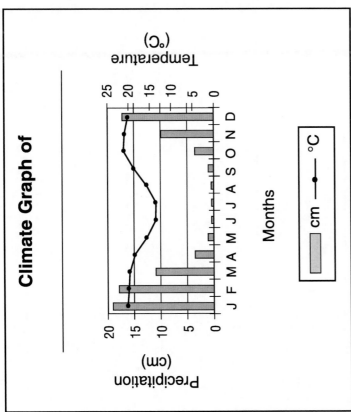

Observations

Climate Graphs *(English)*

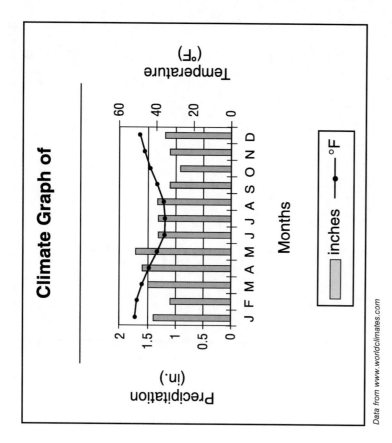

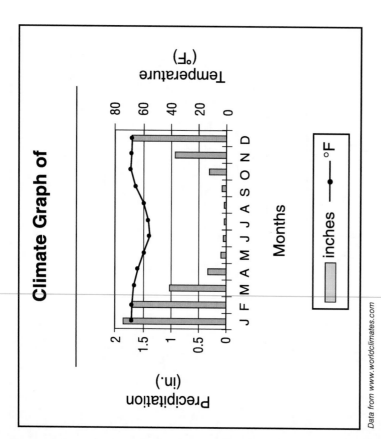

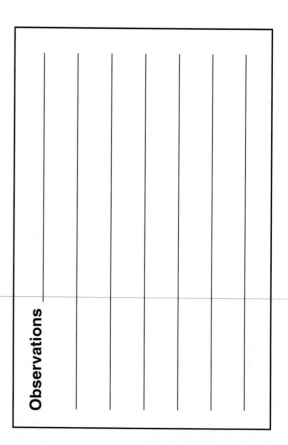

Climate Graphs *(English)* *(cont.)*

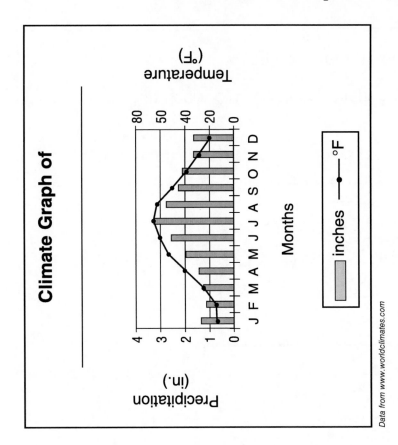

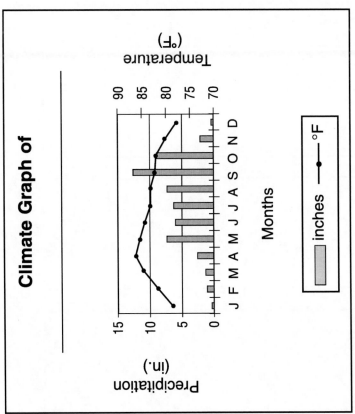

World Climate Regions

1. Label the five lines of latitude on the globe below.

2. Color code the boxes and the map. Use one color each for low, middle, and high latitude.

3. Write the name of each climate region in the correct latitude box.

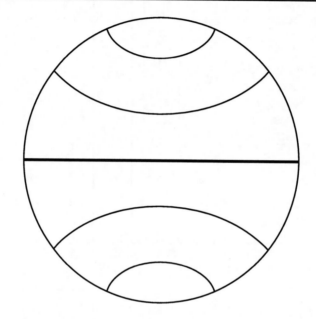

High Latitude Climates

Middle Latitude Climates

Low Latitude Climates

Climate Region Cards

Tropical Humid	**Mediterranean**
Humid Continental	**Humid Subtropical**
Tropical Wet and Dry	**Marine**
Sub-arctic	**Highland**
Arid	**Ice Cap**
Tundra	**Semi-arid**

Climate Notes Key

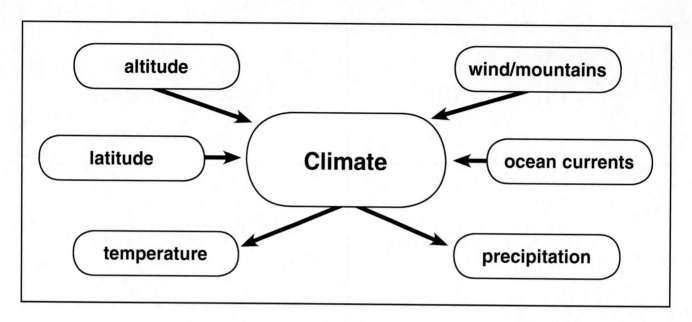

Climate is an area's (*weather pattern over time*). It consists of (*temperature*) and (*precipitation*) (rain, snow, etc.). There are four factors that affect climate. They are (*latitude, altitude, wind/mountains,* and *ocean currents*).

Latitude (distance from the *equator*)
- Climate gets (*colder*) the farther you get from the (*equator*).
- It doesn't matter whether you move (*north*) or (*south*).

Altitude (*height* above sea level)
- Higher altitude = (*cooler, drier*) climate
- Lower altitude = (*warmer, wetter*) climate

Wind and Mountains
- Winds

  From (*ocean*) to (*land*) = "wet" winds. (*Rain*) will fall as air cools.

  From land to ocean = (*dry wind*)

- Mountains

  As wind climbs a mountain, it (*cools*) and causes (*precipitation*). This is the (*windward*) side of the mountain.

  Wind that makes it over the top is (*dried out*). This is the (*leeward*) side of the mountain.

Ocean Currents
- Currents can move (*warm*) or (*cool*) water from one part of the world to another.
- Water warms or cools the (*air*) above it.
- (*Water*) cools and warms slower than (*air*).
- Ocean currents generally make a climate (*milder*).

Climate Graph for Washington, D.C., Key

(*Precipitation*) is shown in (*centimeters*) on the left side of the graph. The (*bar graph*) plots the precipitation.

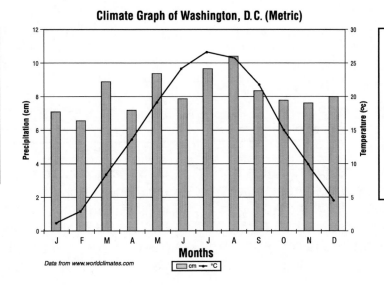

Climate Graph of Washington, D.C. (Metric)

Data from www.worldclimates.com

(*Temperature*) is shown in degrees (*Celsius*) on the right side of the graph. The (*line graph*) plots the temperature.

(*Precipitation*) is shown in (*inches*) on the left side of the graph. The (*bar graph*) plots the precipitation.

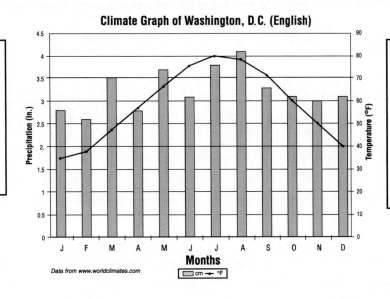

Climate Graph of Washington, D.C. (English)

Data from www.worldclimates.com

(*Temperature*) is shown in degrees (*Fahrenheit*) on the right side of the graph. The (*line graph*) plots the temperature.

Climate Graphs Key *(metric)*

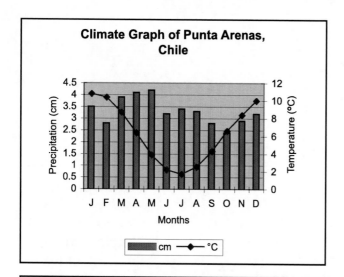

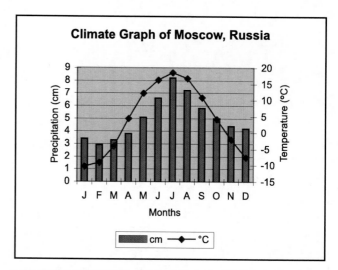

Observations: Temperature indicates a location far from the equator. Reversed seasons (cold in June, July, and August) typical of southern hemisphere. A lot of precipitation. Temperature is cold enough for snow in the winter (June–August).

Observations: Temperature indicates a location far from the equator. The bell-shaped curve of the temperature line indicates an area in the northern hemisphere. A lot of precipitation year-round; snow in the winter.

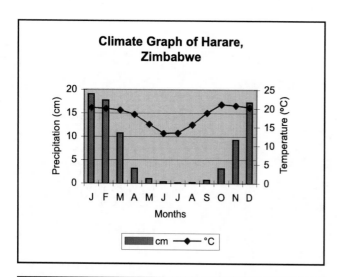

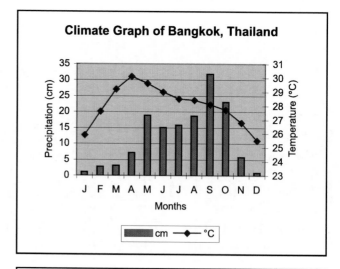

Observations: Cold season in June, July, and August indicates location in the southern hemisphere. Consistently high temperature indicates close to equator. Contrast between wet and dry seasons. May experience droughts in summer.

Observations: Hot season from March through August, typical of northern hemisphere. High average temperatures indicate a country close to the equator. Wet season typical of Southeast Asia (monsoons).

Climate Graphs Key *(English)*

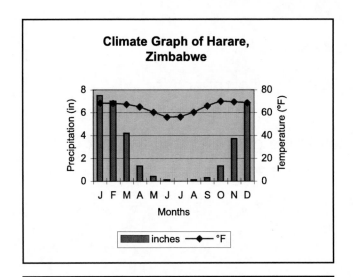

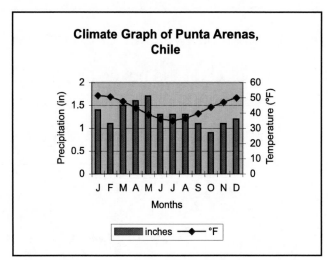

Observations: Cold season in June, July, and August indicates location in the southern hemisphere. Consistently high temperature indicates close to equator. Contrast between wet and dry seasons. May experience droughts in summer.

Observations: Temperature indicates a location far from the equator. Reversed seasons (cold in June, July, and August) typical of southern hemisphere. A lot of precipitation. Temperature is cold enough for snow in the winter (June–August).

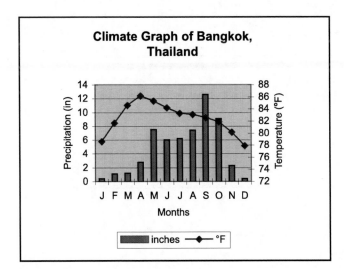

Climate Graph of Moscow, Russia

Observations: Hot season from March through August, typical of northern hemisphere. High average temperatures indicate a country close to the equator. Wet season typical of Southeast Asia (monsoons).

Observations: Temperature indicates a location far from the equator. The bell-shaped curve of the temperature line indicates an area in the northern hemisphere. A lot of precipitation year-round; snow in the winter.

World Climate Regions Key

1. Label the five lines of latitude on the globe below.

2. Color code the boxes and the map. Use one color each for low, middle, and high latitudes.

3. Write the name of each climate region in the correct latitude box.

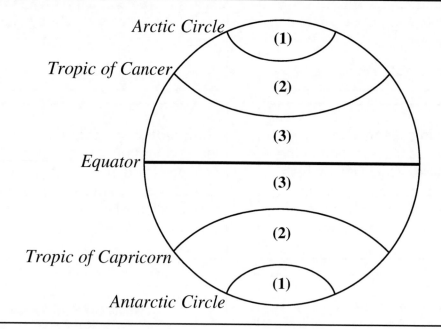

High Latitude Climates (#1 sections/blue)
sub-arctic, arid, tundra, ice cap, semi-arid, highlands

Middle Latitude Climates (#2 sections/yellow)
Mediterranean, humid subtropical, marine west coast, humid continental, arid, semi-arid, highlands

Low Latitude Climates (#3 sections/red)
tropical humid, tropical wet and dry, arid, semi-arid, highlands

Growing Pains

Overview

Students investigate the ties between climate patterns and vegetation. They plant crops to reinforce their knowledge and to infer implications for global hunger. Finally, they create acrostic poems explaining in their own words the connections between climate patterns and vegetation.

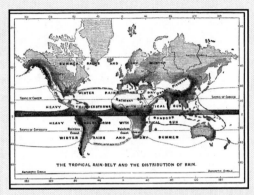

Courtesy of www.clipart.com

The answer key for student reproducibles is located at the end of the lesson. It is helpful for the teacher to examine such keys before beginning the lesson or distributing any reproducibles to the class. This type of advance inspection will (1) improve teacher understanding and presentation, (2) prepare the teacher for possible alternative student responses, (3) help with classroom time management, and (4) result in optimum focus and effectiveness for the activity.

Objectives

- Students will understand the characteristics and uses of spatial organization of Earth's surface.
- Students will understand the characteristics of ecosystems on Earth's surface.

Central Question

How are climate and vegetation connected?

Materials

You will need to prepare and/or provide the following:

- research resources for vegetation (Internet, textbooks, atlas, etc.)
- *Vegetation Cards* (one per student), page 73
- *Vegetation Notes* (one per student), page 74
- *Farmland Grid* (one per group), page 75
- *Climate Region Cards* (three per group), page 76

- overhead transparency of *Crops List*, page 77
- *Review Questions* (optional), page 78
- *Discussion Questions*, page 79
- paper and pencils

Answer Key

Vegetation Notes Key . . . . .page 80

Growing Pains *(cont.)*

Directions

Day One

1. The day before beginning this activity, ask each student to bring in a food item from home. Make sure students have permission to bring the food items and that they understand that these items will be returned. Begin class by asking students to tell the class what food they brought and where it is from (most companies now include this information on the label). You may wish to illustrate this information by putting pins in a world map over each country represented.

2. Discuss with your class that much of what we eat comes from other countries, and they will explore why certain countries grow certain crops and what this means to their economies.

3. Pass out the *Vegetation Cards*. Have students use the research resources to define each vegetation region at least once. They should then record a brief (four- to eight-word) description of each vegetation region and draw a simple sketch.

4. Pass out the *Vegetation Notes* sheet. Have your students cut out their *Vegetation Cards* and glue them into the appropriate zones on the *Vegetation Notes*.

5. Lead a class discussion on the connections between climate (temperature and precipitation) and vegetation. Point out that just as climate zones are related to latitude, so are vegetation regions.

Day Two

1. Explain to students that they will play a game to investigate the effects of climate on a specific type of vegetation or farming. All countries depend on agriculture to feed their people. Some countries are able to produce extra agricultural goods for export and money. Other countries need to import food in order to feed their populations. Whether a country can feed its people without imported food depends largely on location.

2. Divide your class into groups of three to five students. Give each group a *Farmland Grid*, three *Climate Region Cards*, and at least one copy of the irrigation card.

3. Display a copy of *Crops List* on the overhead projector.

4. Ask questions to review previously learned material. You can use *Review Questions* included in this lesson, or you can create your own. Each group that answers a question correctly can "plant" a crop in one square. Students should use the *Crop List* to see what crops they can plant based on their *Climate Region Cards*. Each square equals 100 acres/40 hectares. No single crop can take up more than 500 acres/200 hectares.

5. Check team progress regularly. See that crops correspond to a group's climate conditions. Misplaced crops should be "stricken" with pestilence, disease, or other disaster. At the end, the team with the greatest acreage under cultivation wins.

6. Lead a class discussion, using the *Discussion Questions*.

7. *Arts Integration:* Have students create acrostic poems using the word "vegetation" to explain the connections between climate and vegetation. (An acrostic poem spells out a word vertically, while the lines of the poem run horizontally. Acrostics do not have to rhyme.) You may wish to have your students illustrate their poems.

Vegetation Cards

Desert	**Desert**	**Desert**
Description:	Description:	Description:
Sketch:	Sketch:	Sketch:

Desert	**Desert**	**Tundra**
Description:	Description:	Description:
Sketch:	Sketch:	Sketch:

Tundra	**Coniferous Forest**	**Coniferous Forest**
Description:	Description:	Description:
Sketch:	Sketch:	Sketch:

Tropical Rainforest	**Temperate Rainforest**	**Temperate Rainforest**
Description:	Description:	Description:
Sketch:	Sketch:	Sketch:

Prairie	**Prairie**	**Savanna**
Description:	Description:	Description:
Sketch:	Sketch:	Sketch:

Vegetation Notes

High Latitude

Middle Latitude

Low Latitude

Middle Latitude

High Latitude

Farmland Grid

Climate Region Cards

Tropical Humid	**Mediterranean**
Humid Continental	**Humid Subtropical**
Tropical Wet and Dry	**Marine**
Semi-arid	**Highland**
Arid	**Irrigation**

Crops List

Tropical Humid	**Humid Subtropical**
coconuts	cotton
bananas	rice
rice	sugar cane
teak	tea
mahogany	peanuts
	vegetables
Marine	citrus fruits
wheat	
sugar beets	**Semi-arid**
orchards	vegetables*
vegetables	citrus fruits*
corn	
rye	**Humid Continental**
	vegetables
Tropical Wet and Dry	potatoes
corn	corn
millet	wheat
beans	soybeans
wheat	oats
	orchards
Mediterranean	
olives	**Highland**
grapes	tea
citrus fruits	coffee
fig	cotton
wheat*	
vegetables*	**Arid**
	vegetables*
	citrus fruits*

*These crops may only be grown with irrigation.

Review Questions

1. What is an archipelago?
2. What is a river source?
3. What is a river mouth?
4. What is a tributary?
5. What is a mountain range?
6. What is an isthmus?
7. What is a strait?
8. What is a desert?
9. What is an oasis?
10. What is a bay?
11. What is a gulf?
12. What is a harbor?
13. What is a canal?
14. What is a tundra?
15. What is a glacier?
16. What is a plateau?
17. What is a volcano?
18. What is a delta?
19. What is a peninsula?
20. What is a cape?
21. What is a river?
22. What is an atoll?
23. What is a lagoon?
24. What is a river branch?
25. What is the purpose of a map scale?
26. What is the purpose of a compass rose?
27. What is the purpose of a map title?
28. What is the purpose of a legend/key?

29. What is latitude?
30. What is longitude?
31. What is the equator?
32. What is the prime meridian?
33. What are parallels?
34. What are meridians?
35. Which comes first—latitude or longitude?
36. Where on a map do you find the numbers for latitude?
37. Where on a map do you find the numbers for longitude?
38. What is climate?
39. What are the two parts of climate?
40. Name the four factors that contribute to climate.
41. What does the bar graph on a climate graph show?
42. What does the line graph on a climate graph show?
43. What information goes on the bottom of a climate graph?
44. Name a climate found in low latitudes.
45. Name a climate found in middle latitudes.
46. Name a climate found in high latitudes.
47. What is a savanna?
48. What is a deciduous forest?
49. What is a coniferous forest?
50. What is agriculture?

Discussion Questions

1. Were any groups able to cultivate all of their acreage?

   (No country uses all of its land for farming, and many countries have little or no arable land.)

2. How many groups had poor climates for growing food?

   (Many countries have poor climates for growing food, and they depend on imports to feed their populations.)

3. Which climates were the most productive?

   (Middle latitude climates usually have the largest range of crops.)

4. What effect does climate have on a country's ability to provide food for its people?

   (Climate determines what and how much food a country can produce. However, if the country has the resources, it can employ technology to increase its food production.)

5. How can irrigation help a country with poor climate?

   (Irrigation is one form of technology that can increase a country's food production.)

6. Make a generalization about the connections between climate and vegetation.

   (Answers will vary but should include the fact that certain plants need certain conditions in which to flourish. Many agricultural products cannot survive in extreme climates without the intervention of technology. Yet people live in all of the climates included in this activity. That means that some populations depend on technology and trade to get enough food for the people.)

Vegetation Notes Key

High Latitude

Tundra	Desert
mosses/ lichens that can survive freezing	vegetation that doesn't need much precipitation

Middle Latitude

Prairie	Temperate Rainforest	Coniferous Forest	Desert
dense grasses and clusters of trees	tall, old-growth trees	evergreen trees and shrubs	vegetation that doesn't need much precipitation

Low Latitude

Savanna	Tropical Rainforest	Desert
sparse grass and scrubby trees	jungle-like vegetation; dense undergrowth	vegetation that doesn't need much precipitation

Middle Latitude

Prairie	Temperate Rainforest	Coniferous Forest	Desert
dense grasses and clusters of trees	tall, old-growth trees	evergreen trees and shrubs	vegetation that doesn't need much precipitation

High Latitude

Tundra	Desert
mosses/ lichens that can survive freezing	vegetation that doesn't need much precipitation

Rock Your World

Overview

This lesson was created by Diana Jordan of Kenmore Middle School in Arlington, Virginia. Students investigate four types of plate movement—convergence, divergence, subduction, and faulting—through the use of a puzzle and class readings. Then they use simple movement to create skits of plate movement and its effects on the physical environment.

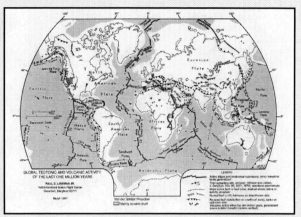

Courtesy of Paul D. Lowman Jr./NASA

The answer key for student reproducibles is located at the end of the lesson. It is helpful for the teacher to examine such keys before beginning the lesson or distributing any reproducibles to the class. This type of advance inspection will (1) improve teacher understanding and presentation, (2) prepare the teacher for possible alternative student responses, (3) help with classroom time management, and (4) result in optimum focus and effectiveness for the activity.

Objective

- Students will know and understand the physical processes that shape patterns on Earth's surface.

Central Question

How do plate tectonics affect the physical environment?

Materials

You will need to prepare and/or provide the following:

- textbook or other readings on plate tectonics
- *Plate Movement Chart* (one per student), page 83
- *Plate Tectonics Puzzle* (one per group), page 84
- video/still camera (optional)

Answer Key

Plate Movement Chart Key. . . . . .page 85

Rock Your World *(cont.)*

Directions

Day One

1. The day before this activity, assign a textbook or other reading to your students and have them complete the first three columns of the *Plate Movement Chart* (sketch, definition, and results). Students should also define plate tectonics in their own words at the bottom of the page.

2. Before class, copy and cut out enough *Plate Tectonics Puzzles* for your class (one per group).

3. Begin class by having student volunteers share their definitions of plate tectonics. Come to a consensus as a class of a clear, concise definition.

4. Put your students into groups of three or four to assemble the *Plate Tectonics Puzzle*. Use the following questions to guide your students:

   • What does this show? *(Earth's plates and their movements)*

   • Where would the equator be? *(in the middle)*

   • What do the arrows represent? Why are they different lengths? *(They represent the direction in which plates move. Longer arrows indicate faster movement, and shorter arrows indicate slower movement.)*

5. Review students' responses to the first three columns of the *Plate Movement Chart*. Ask for volunteers to find examples of each type of movement on the a map of the world. For example, your students should be able to tell you that subduction occurs when a heavy ocean plate meets a lighter continental plate and slides under it. An example of subduction can be found where the Nazca plate meets the South American plate, forming the Andes Mountains. Students should add the examples found as a class to their notes in the far-right column.

Day Two

1. *Arts Integration:* Divide your students into groups of four or five. Assign each group a type of plate movement. You may have more than one group for each type.

2. Your students will act out their assigned plate movements. Each group will create a skit that acts out its plate movement and will freeze at the final part of the skit. The skit should show the actual plate movement and the resulting landforms.

3. The class watches the skits and guesses the types of plate movement. The student who identifies each movement must explain how the skit showed this type of movement.

4. You may wish to videotape or photograph each of the skits. Use the photos with other classes as additional practice. You could create "plate stations" with the photos, where students can identify the type of plate movement and choose one photo that they think best represents the movement and why.

5. Lead a class discussion answering the central question, "How do plate tectonics affect the physical environment?"

Plate Movement Chart

The following chart lists the four major ways that Earth's plates move.

Name and Sketch	Definition	Results of Movement	Examples
Spreading/ Diverging			
Converging			
Subduction			
Faulting			

Definition of plate tectonics: _____

_____

_____

Plate Tectonics Puzzle

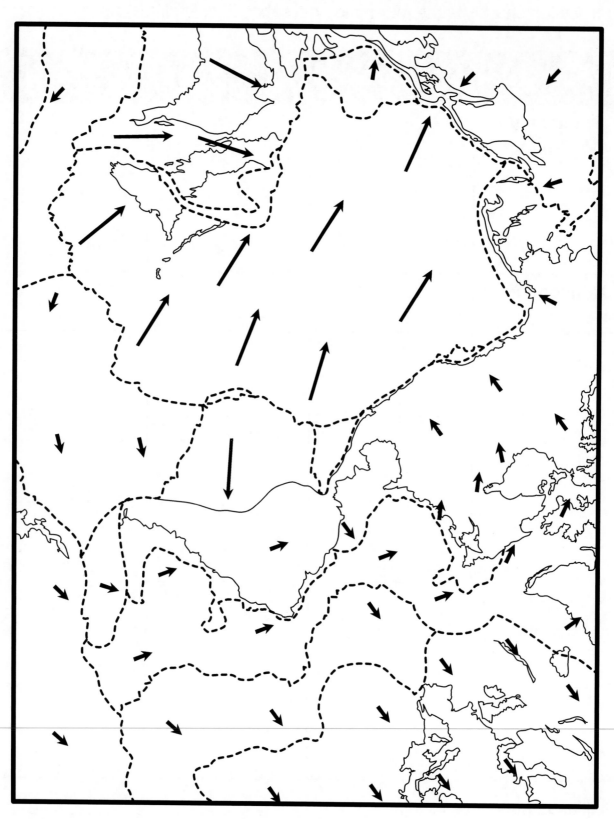

Plate tectonics puzzle from the USGS website:

http://quake.wr.usgs.gov/research/deformation/modeling/teaching/puzzle/puzzle_letter.gif

Plate Movement Chart Key

Name and Sketch	Definition	Results of Movement	Example
Spreading/ Diverging ← →	two plates that move away from each other; usually oceanic plates	oceanic ridge (if they are oceanic plates)	Mid-Atlantic Ridge ; Iceland is part of it.
		rift valley if on land can cause earthquakes and volcanoes	The Great Rift Valley, East Africa
Converging ↗ ↖	two plates that move towards each other; usually land plates	mountain ranges	Himalaya Mountains in South Asia; They grow about one inch/2.54 cm per year.
Subduction	two oceanic plates that meet and move downwards	trenches	Mariana Trench in the Pacific Ocean (lowest point on Earth's surface 35,802 ft/10,912.45 m)
	one oceanic and one land plate: heavier oceanic plate moves under land plate	lower mountain ranges and volcanoes	Andes Mountains in South America
Faulting ↑ ↓	two plates that slide past each other sideways; can be land or oceanic	earthquakes along fault lines	San Andreas Fault in California

Definition of plate tectonics: *Answers will vary but should include the fact that Earth's crust is made up of large pieces that move. This means that Earth's surface is constantly changing.*

There's Trouble Brewin'

Overview

In this activity, students identify the causes and effects of various natural disasters and how human beings adapt to places that are susceptible to these events. Students create trading cards of natural disasters and then play a game to collect a complete set of cards.

Courtesy of www.clipart.com

The answer key for student reproducibles is located at the end of the lesson. It is helpful for the teacher to examine such keys before beginning the lesson or distributing any reproducibles to the class. This type of advance inspection will (1) improve teacher understanding and presentation, (2) prepare the teacher for possible alternative student responses, (3) help with classroom time management, and (4) result in optimum focus and effectiveness for the activity.

Objectives

- Students will know the physical processes that shape patterns on Earth's surface.

Central Question

How do human beings adapt to natural disasters?

Materials

You will need to prepare and/or provide the following:

- overhead transparency of *Natural Disasters Matrix*, pages 88–89
- *Natural Disasters Matrix* (one per student), pages 88–89
- one set of the *Natural Disasters Information* sheets, pages 90–98
- *Trading Cards Template* (cut apart) (optional), page 99
- *Mystery Disaster Description* (cut apart; one per student), page 100
- large construction paper

Answer Key

Natural Disasters Matrix Key. . . . . pages 101–102

There's Trouble Brewin' *(cont.)*

Directions

Day One

1. Before class, photocopy one set of the *Natural Disasters Information* pages and attach them to large construction paper to create posters. You do not have to use the entire set, but you will need posters for the natural disasters that you address in your class. Place these posters around the room where students can sit comfortably in small groups of three or four. Number each station so that your students know where to start.

2. Arrange your students in groups of three or four. Give each student a copy of the *Natural Disasters Matrix*.

3. Assign each group a number that corresponds to a station. Tell your students that they will begin their research at the station with the same number. They have to rotate through the stations taking notes on each disaster.

4. Give your students five to ten minutes at each station. Then, rotate groups to the next station.

5. With about 15 minutes left in class, bring your students back to their seats and go over their answers by asking volunteers to fill in the overhead copy of the *Natural Disasters Matrix*.

Day Two

1. *Arts Integration:* Your students will create trading cards about natural disasters. Trading cards contain concise information as well as a clear visual image. They will use these cards to play a game.

2. Assign each group a natural disaster. Each group will create a class set of trading cards for that disaster. For example, if you have 24 students and they are working in groups of four, each student in the hurricane group would create six hurricane trading cards. You may wish to give each group the corresponding poster from the day before.

3. The trading cards should include a picture and the name of the disaster on one side, and the regions, causes, effects, and ways people adapt to it on the other. Remind your students to be concise in their descriptions, and to create clear visual images. You may wish to use the *Trading Cards Template* with your students.

4. When all of the groups are finished, distribute the *Mystery Disaster Description*. Each group should create a short written description of its disaster (without naming the disaster). Each group member will need a copy of this description.

5. Jigsaw your students so that there is one member from each disaster group in the new groups.

6. Students take turns reading their descriptions. The other members of the jigsaw group must use their knowledge from the day before to guess which disaster is being described. Those students who guess correctly receive one of the trading cards of that disaster from the person who created them. You may wish to allow students to use their *Natural Disasters Matrix*.

7. The goal of the game is to acquire a complete set of trading cards. You may wish to have an incentive available to students who complete their sets. See page 176 for *Incentive Suggestions*.

Natural Disasters Matrix

Disaster	Affected Regions	Causes	Effects and Adaptations

Natural Disasters Matrix *(cont)*

Disaster	Affected Regions	Causes	Effects and Adaptations

Natural Disasters Information: Hurricane

Hurricanes are storms created over large bodies of water when a warm-air mass collides with a cool-air mass. In parts of the Pacific Ocean, hurricanes are called typhoons. A hurricane forms a circular storm, with a calm center called an eye. In order for a storm to be considered a hurricane, its winds must blow at 74 miles (119 km) per hour or more.

Hurricanes can last more than two weeks over the water. Most hurricanes that form in the Atlantic Ocean threaten Caribbean islands and the southeastern United States, although some hurricanes can travel up the entire eastern coast. Usually, however, the storms that travel that far do not reach land. They stay over the ocean and eventually run out of energy as they reach colder and colder waters.

Hurricanes can cause much destruction. The storm itself can bring heavy rains, high winds, and large storm surges. (A storm surge is a rise in sea level that affects coastal areas and areas along rivers.) The results of these effects are flooding, downed power lines and tree limbs, power outages, and damage to buildings. In 2005, a large Hurricane Katrina caused billions of dollars of damage to the Gulf States in the United States.

People have long lived in areas that get hit by hurricanes. In many of these areas, there are established evacuation routes, marked by roadside signs. In addition, there are hurricane warning systems in place to let people know that the storm is coming so that they can leave before it hits. Another way that people adapt to hurricane-prone areas is to build houses on stilts. The stilts keep the homes above the level of the rising water and limit the damage to the homes. Once a hurricane is on its way, many people board up their homes and businesses to protect them.

Courtesy of www.photos.com

Natural Disasters Information: Tornado

A tornado is a windstorm that occurs over land. Like a hurricane, it is caused by the collision of a warm-air mass and a cool-air mass. However, tornadoes usually form over land. Tornadoes that form over water are called waterspouts, and they are usually weak compared to the land versions. Tornadoes often occur with thunderstorms and can be caused by hurricanes.

A tornado is a funnel-shaped cloud that moves erratically (unevenly) across the ground. A tornado can move fast or slow, and it can "jump" from one area to another. Tornadoes can cause widespread destruction in a very short time. Winds in a tornado can reach up to 300 miles (483 km) per hour. The typical tornado—gray or black in color—is actually a combination of the tornado's winds (which have no color) and the debris that the tornado has picked up along its route (dust, dirt, etc.).

Courtesy of www.clipart.com

Tornadoes form over flat land where they can pick up speed. "Tornado Alley" is a term used to refer to the central plains states. This is an area extending from Nebraska southward through Kansas and Oklahoma into central Texas. States in this area are at the greatest risk for tornadoes. Tornadoes can occur anywhere in the world. However, the United States by far suffers the greatest damage from tornadoes each year. The largest tornado in U.S. history was the tri-state tornado of March 18, 1925. It killed almost 700 people.

Because tornadoes are hard to predict and track, there is not a lot that people can do to prepare for them. Evacuating an area after a tornado has been spotted, or heading to a safe place such as a basement or "safe room" (a specially constructed tornado-proof room) are people's only options.

Natural Disaster Information: Flood

Floods are rising water levels that overflow their usual boundaries. Flooding can occur in rivers or along coastlines. Low-lying areas near large bodies of water are especially at risk for flooding on a regular basis, but any area can experience flooding under the right conditions.

Flooding is caused by an increase in the volume of water in an area. The increase can be caused by heavy rains or by rapid melting of snow in higher areas. Water levels can rise quickly or slowly, depending on the source. In general, it takes a few days for flood conditions to occur, so there is usually plenty of warning time.

Flooding can cause water damage to buildings, including damage from mold and mildew. In addition, flooding can erode coastlines and river banks, taking away from the total land available for people's use.

Because flooding usually takes several days to occur, people can prepare for floods. Placing sandbags along river banks can help contain rising water. As with hurricane areas, some people in flood-prone areas build their houses on stilts to prevent water damage. In the case of flash flooding (really fast flooding), people's only option is to evacuate the area as fast as possible. In 2005, Hurricane Katrina damaged New Orleans's protection from the high waters. New Orleans was flooded and many parts of the city were destroyed.

Courtesy of www.photos.com

Natural Disasters Information: Blizzard

A blizzard is a winter storm with high winds and drifting or falling snow. Drifts can reach several feet above the actual snowfall. For example, if a snow storm drops 7 feet (2.13 meters) of snow, drifts during a blizzard may reach as high as 12 feet (3.66 meters). Cold temperatures and low wind chills (how cold it feels with the wind, as opposed to the actual temperature) accompany blizzards.

Blizzards are caused by a high-pressure system, which may bring snow, followed by a low-pressure system, which brings wind. Because of the blowing snow, visibility may become limited. This makes driving very dangerous. In a blizzard, it is best to stay indoors if at all possible because of the limited visibility and the wind chill.

Courtesy of www.photos.com

Areas that commonly receive blizzards are those areas in middle to high latitudes. Areas near lakes can also receive "lake-effect" snows during blizzards. Lake effect means a sudden, heavy snowfall which results from the warmer, wetter air over the lake meeting the colder, drier air above it.

Like floods, there is usually a fair amount of warning with blizzards. To prepare for a blizzard, people get their shoveling supplies (shovels, snow blowers, bags of salt) and stock up on supplies such as food and batteries. It is also important to prevent the pipes in a house from freezing by wrapping them to insulate them and by leaving the taps open just a little.

In February 2006, 26.9 inches of snow fell on New York City. The city was prepared though. The students in the city went to school the very next day!

Natural Disasters Information: Wildfire

Wildfires are fires that usually begin in uninhabited areas of forest and eventually reach areas where people live. Wildfires can burn along the forest floor or among the tops of the trees, but the result is the same: acres of destroyed wildlife and vegetation and ruined homes.

NPS Photo by Jeff Henry

Unlike most natural disasters, wildfires are most often started by the carelessness of human beings. Campfires that have not been properly put out and cigarettes or matches tossed in the woods start many of the nation's wildfires. Lightning can cause wildfires, too, which is why they are considered a natural disaster. Far more frequently, however, it is people who cause these huge, destructive fires.

Wildfires can occur anywhere there are people and vegetation, but they are more frequent in dry areas, especially areas experiencing drought. Forests and scrub vegetation (vegetation found in desert areas) are most at risk for wildfires.

These fires destroy the area's vegetation and wildlife, scorching the earth and making it difficult for new vegetation to grow. They also ruin people's homes. As with other types of fire, the best measures people can take to prepare for wildfires is to try to prevent them. Making sure campfires are completely doused, along with refraining from smoking in forest areas, goes a long way in preventing forest fires. In addition, people can use fire-resistant materials to build their homes. Stone walls and patios, along with swimming pools, can help to reduce the risk of fire damage to a home.

In the summer of 1988, there was a huge wildfire in Yellowstone National Park. Actually, it was fires all burning at the same time. Almost 25,000 people helped stop the fires. This was the largest firefighting effort in United States history.

Natural Disasters Information: Drought

A drought is a long period of time with little or no precipitation. In temperate regions, a drought is defined as 15 days in a row with less than 0.01 inches of rain. Most areas experience short periods of drought during a year. But when a drought goes on for months or years, it spells disaster for the people who live there. Areas such as those surrounding deserts are most at risk for drought conditions.

Droughts can cause widespread destruction of people, wildlife, and vegetation. Without enough water to grow crops, people suffer from starvation. In addition, water is necessary for all life. Without an adequate supply, plants, animals, and people are all at risk of dying. Dust storms are also created when the region's vegetation dies off. There are no longer any plants to hold the soil in place, and erosion takes over. Cracks form on the surface of the earth when there is not enough water to keep it whole.

People can prepare for droughts by rationing (or limiting) their use of water. In areas of extreme, extended drought, irrigation systems can be put into place. Organizations such as the Peace Corps send volunteers to areas suffering from extended drought to help local people build and run such systems. Other nations also help drought-affected areas by sending food supplies.

The states in the West have been in a drought for many years. In fact, the U.S. Geological Survey claims this is the worst drought in United States history.

Courtesy of www.photos.com

Natural Disasters Information: Tsunami

A tsunami is a huge ocean or sea wave, caused by an underwater disturbance. Earthquakes, volcanic eruptions, and mudslides under the ocean or sea floor can cause tsunamis. On the shoreline, you can see the water recede (pull back) before a tsunami hits. While this action can warn people that a tsunami is about to hit, it does not leave much time to prepare.

Areas along the coast of an ocean or sea are at risk for a tsunami. This is especially true in the Pacific Rim, where the Ring of Fire frequently experiences underwater earthquakes and volcanoes. Tsunamis are more frequent in the Pacific Ocean than in any other ocean, although some of the largest tsunamis, such as the one on December 26, 2004, have occurred in the Indian Ocean. Tsunamis have wreaked havoc on coastal areas in all of Earth's oceans and seas.

Courtesy of www.clipart.com

Tsunamis cause erosion of the coastline, as well as heavy flooding, sometimes miles inland. In areas of the Pacific Ocean, there is a tsunami warning system in place, much like a hurricane warning system. An alarm goes off to warn residents of an impending tsunami. Once warned, people's only course of action is to evacuate the area, heading inland for higher ground.

Tsunami in Hawaii, 1946
Courtesy of the National Oceanic and Atmospheric Administration/Department of Commerce

Natural Disasters Information: Earthquake

Earthquakes are disturbances under Earth's surface that can result in violent shaking and swaying of the surface. They are caused when two plates slide past each other. This type of plate movement is called *faulting*. In the United States, one of the most famous fault lines is the San Andreas Fault in California. Earthquakes can also be caused by diverging plates, such as along the Great Rift Valley in eastern Africa.

Because Earth's surface is made up of many moving plates, earthquakes are felt throughout the world. Only about one-fifth of all the world's earthquakes are strong enough to be felt by people. Of those that can be felt by people, only about one out of a thousand cause noticeable damage.

Earthquakes, as the name suggests, cause the ground to shake and sway. Buildings can sometimes collapse in a strong earthquake; however, many buildings in areas where earthquakes are frequent are built in a way that minimizes damage to the building. For example, large buildings in Tokyo are built on giant springs or rollers that absorb some of the movement from the quakes. Earthquakes can open up the ground, and they can also cause tsunamis if they occur underwater.

People can try to evacuate an area if an earthquake is occurring, but since it is difficult to predict earthquakes, there is not usually much time to plan an escape. The safest place to wait out an earthquake is under a reinforced piece of furniture (such as a large table) if there is one nearby. It is not wise to try to move to another location during an earthquake.

Earthquake damage in Alaska, 1964
Courtesy of the National Oceanic and Atmospheric
Administration/Department of Commerce

Natural Disasters Information: Volcano

Volcanic eruptions are blasts of fiery lava and rock from deep below Earth's surface. They can create huge clouds of hot ash that travel many miles from the original eruption. In addition, volcanic eruptions can cause fires, mudslides, earthquakes, and even tsunamis if the eruption occurs underwater.

Areas that are prone to volcanic eruptions are those along subducting or diverging plate boundaries. The Pacific Ring of Fire is a particularly active volcanic area, due to the many plate boundaries surrounding the area.

Evacuation continues to be the best way to prepare for an eruption. However, volcanoes can be hard to predict. Sometimes a volcano will give signs that it is about to erupt. In those cases, leaving the area immediately is the best way to prepare. When evacuating an area near a volcano, people look for higher ground that is upwind of the volcano (the wind blows from the person toward the volcano). Once out of the area, people have little to do but wait for the eruption to stop.

As with wildfires, using fire-resistant building materials can increase the chances for a building or home to survive a volcanic eruption. Pools, patios, and stone walls can help keep hot lava flows and fires from destroying property.

Courtesy of www.photos.com

Trading Cards Template

Front

Name of Disaster

_____

Picture

Back

Regions: _____
_____

Causes: _____
_____
_____

Effects: _____
_____

Adaptations: _____
_____
_____
_____

Front

Name of Disaster

_____

Picture

Back

Regions: _____
_____

Causes: _____
_____
_____

Effects: _____
_____

Adaptations: _____
_____
_____
_____

Mystery Disaster Description

Describe your group's disaster here. Be sure not to use the name of your disaster!

_____

_____

_____

_____

_____

Describe your group's disaster here. Be sure not to use the name of your disaster!

_____

_____

_____

_____

_____

Describe your group's disaster here. Be sure not to use the name of your disaster!

_____

_____

_____

_____

_____

Natural Disasters Matrix Key

Disaster	Regions	Causes	Effects and Adaptations
Hurricane	Caribbean islands, southeast coastal United States	warm-air currents meeting cold-air currents over warm water	high winds; heavy rains; storm surges
			hurricane warning systems; boarding up homes; evacuation; homes on stilts
Flood	any low-lying area or coastal area	long, heavy rains or sudden snow thawing	water damage to property; erosion of coastlines and river banks
			houses on stilts; sandbagging of river banks; evacuation
Tornado	Central United States ("Tornado Alley")	warm- and cold-air currents meeting over land; can be caused by hurricane or thunderstorm	funnel-shaped wind cloud with very fast winds; can move fast or slow
			going to low ground (a cellar) or a safe room; evacuation
Blizzard	middle to high latitudes (north and south)	high-pressure system followed by low-pressure system	strong winds; high drifts of snow; heavy snowfall can occur
			shovels, bags of salt, and snow blowers ready; remaining inside during blizzards
Wildfire	dry areas with forest or scrub vegetation	sometimes lightning; more often human carelessness	scorched earth, destruction of homes, wildlife, and vegetation; dense smoke
			use fire-resistant building materials; evacuation

Natural Disasters Matrix Key *(cont.)*

Disaster	Regions	Causes	Effects and Adaptations
Drought	anywhere, especially areas around deserts	lack of rainfall for extended periods of time	destruction of crops; lack of food for people and wildlife; cracked earth; dust storms
			irrigation systems; food aid from other countries; water rationing
Tsunami	ocean and coastal areas	underwater disturbance like earthquake, volcano eruption, or mudslide	huge waves that destroy coastal areas; erosion of coast; heavy flooding
			tsunami warning system (Pacific Ocean only); evacuation—head inland for higher ground
Earthquake	areas along faulting plate boundaries	faulting (two plates sliding past each other)	ground shaking; buildings collapse; cracks in the earth opening up; tsunamis
			buildings built to prevent damage (springs, rollers); staying put; getting under solid cover
Volcano	areas near subducting plates; the Pacific "Ring of Fire"	subducting (one plate sliding under another) or diverging (plates moving away from each other)	hot liquid lava and ash; explosion of rocks; fires, mudslides, earthquakes, tsunamis
			fire-resistant building materials; evacuation—avoiding low-lying areas, staying upwind of volcano

Water, Water, Everywhere

Overview

In this activity, students analyze the importance of access to fresh water for everyday life. Students take a virtual tour of some of the world's most water-stressed areas, answer questions about access and availability, and then create news reports highlighting some of the issues surrounding the world's fresh water.

The answer key for student reproducibles is located at the end of the lesson. It is helpful for the teacher to examine such keys before beginning the lesson or distributing any reproducibles to the class. This type of advance inspection will (1) improve teacher understanding and presentation, (2) prepare the teacher for possible alternative student responses, (3) help with classroom time management, and (4) result in optimum focus and effectiveness for the activity.

Courtesy of www.photos.com

Objective

- Students will understand the characteristics of ecosystems on Earth's surface.

Central Question

How vital are water issues to world geography, and how do humans adapt to these issues?

Materials

You will need to prepare and/or provide the following:

- research resources on water (Internet, textbooks, atlas, etc.)
- *Tour Stops* (one class set), pages 105–111
- *World Water Tour* (one per student), pages 112–113
- overhead transparency of *World Water Tour*,

- pages 112–113
- *News Report Roles Sheet* (one per group), page 114
- *Water Research Questions* (one per group), page 115
- video camera (optional)

Answer Key

World Water Tour Key . . . . pages 116–117

Water, Water, Everywhere *(cont.)*

Directions

Day One

1. Before class, display the seven *Tour Stops* sheets around your room.

2. Divide your class into groups of three or four students and distribute copies of *World Water Tour*.

3. Give your students ample time to complete the tour of the world's water issues (20–30 minutes). Make sure that your students understand that some of the questions on the tour have no correct answers and that any reasonable answer will be accepted, provided it is supported with facts.

4. Go over your students' answers, using the overhead copy of the *World Water Tour* and the suggested answers on pages 116–117.

Day Two

1. *Arts Integration:* Your students will create news reports covering one of the issues they read about on their tour. A news report is brief, to the point, and often includes a human interest angle.

2. Divide your class into groups of four or five students.

3. Assign each group a water issue to cover. Possible topics might include these:
   - China's Three Gorges Dam
   - Turkey's Ataturk Dam (or other dams)
   - Israel and Jordan (the Jordan River)
   - Spain's southern coast
   - The Oglala Aquifer
   - Egypt and its neighbors (sharing the Nile)
   - Iraq's disappearing wetlands
   - The Aral Sea
   - Lake Chad
   - Mexico City
   - Ganges River (depletion and pollution)
   - Southern Australia (Darling and Murray Rivers)

4. Each person in the group should have a role. You may wish to assign roles or allow your students to choose roles after reading the *News Report Roles Sheet*.

5. Give your students time to research their issues. The newscast should include answers to all of the *Water Research Questions*.

6. If time and resources permit, you may wish to videotape your students' newscasts. The videotapes could then be broadcast within the school or in the local media. You may wish to coordinate this activity with your English or drama teacher.

7. Complete the activity by discussing the central question from page 103.

Tour Stop 1: The Earth's Water Supply

Over 70% of Earth is made up of water. This may seem like plenty of water to sustain a growing population, but consider how this water is allocated. Approximately 97% of Earth's water is salt water contained in our oceans and seas. People cannot drink salt water, nor can crops grow in it. This means that only about 3% of Earth's water is fresh water. Of that 3%, almost 70% is found in polar icecaps. Close to 30% of the earth's fresh water can be found either in soil as moisture or in deep underground aquifers. Aquifers are underground reservoirs of ancient or fossil water. These aquifers cannot easily be refilled. It takes millions of years for an aquifer to form. So, all these numbers mean that less than 1% of the world's fresh water is available for human beings in the form of rivers, lakes, above-ground reservoirs, and accessible aquifers. This is the water that is renewed in the hydrological cycle.

The hydrological cycle, or water cycle, explains the changes that water goes through in moving from gas to liquid to solid. Water is in constant motion. Surface water evaporates when its temperature increases. It rises as it gets warmer, and it eventually gets so high that it cools. When it cools, it falls back to the earth in the form of precipitation (rain and snow, mainly). The precipitation rejoins the rivers, lakes, reservoirs, and icecaps on the surface of Earth. When people talk about water as a renewable resource, they are referring to the fact that evaporated water returns to the surface. New water, though, is not created. The amount of water on Earth is almost the same as it was billions of years ago.

Mont Rolland, Quebec

Courtesy of www.photos.com

Tour Stop 2: Ancient Civilizations and Water

All of the world's ancient civilizations developed around sources of fresh water. Water is essential to human survival. About 12,000 years ago, hunter-gatherer societies began to realize that certain places had reliable sources of water. As these groups became larger and less nomadic, they settled in fertile river valleys and near lakes.

With settlement came agriculture, and these groups learned to farm their food, rather than collecting it from the wild. In times of water shortage, people began to use irrigation (diverting water from rivers and lakes to fields) to save their crops and feed their families. Eventually, humankind became so good at creating irrigation systems that they are now used throughout the world in areas where there is not enough precipitation to sustain agriculture.

Ancient civilizations rose up all over the world. Some settled along river banks such as the Fertile Crescent in Mesopotamia and the Nile River Valley in Egypt. Other civilizations, like the Aztecs, established lakeside settlements. In all cases, early humans clearly saw the importance of fresh water for their survival.

Ancient Civilizations and Fresh Water

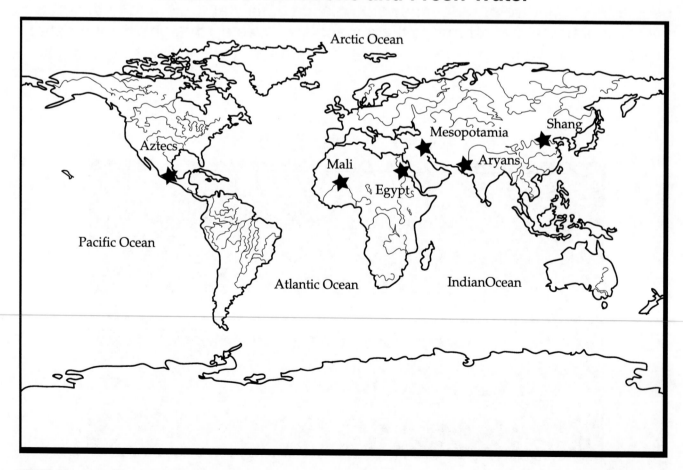

Tour Stop 3: Water and Population

In 1999, the world's population reached six billion people. The world's population continues to grow by about 75 million people yearly. In the last 100 years, the population almost tripled. At the same time, water use increased over six times. As the world's population grows, pressure on already-stressed fresh water systems increases.

People require about 13 gallons (50 liters) of water per day to survive, according to the United Nations (UN). This amount is the minimum required for cooking, washing, drinking, and sanitation. Americans use more water than any other country on Earth. (Per capita, Americans use 158 gallons [600 liters] per day). The average European uses on average 66–92 gallons (250–350 liters) per day, while many people in Sub-Saharan Africa survive on less than 6.5 gallons (25 liters) per day. Currently, one out of three people in the world live in countries that struggle to provide the UN's minimum amount of water. With the world population growing at its current rate, that number could possibly soar to two out of three people by 2025.

The growing population affects water usage in other ways, too. As the population increases, pollution becomes a bigger problem. Five million people die each year as a result of water-borne disease. In addition, 70% of the water used worldwide is used for agriculture. This number will continue to rise as the population increases, causing the need for more food.

Ganges River, India

Courtesy of www.photos.com

Text adapted from *Planet Under Pressure* (BBC)

Tour Stop 4: Aquifer Depletion

Aquifers are underground reservoirs that were filled millions of years ago. Most aquifers are too deep in the ground to be used by humans. But, some are close enough to Earth's surface to be accessible. These sources of fresh water are not usually replenished by precipitation, so they are limited resources. Some countries rely on aquifers for fresh water. The United States and Mexico are two such countries.

The Oglala Reservoir reaches from South Dakota to Texas, covering a span of 800 miles (1,287 km). It provides approximately one third of the water that the United States uses for crop irrigation. Because the aquifer has been cut off from its original source, it is shrinking, and may dry up in as little as 60 years.

Mexico City relies heavily on the aquifers below it for water. Almost 80% of Mexico City's water comes from underground sources. These aquifers have been so depleted that the city is actually sinking. It has sunk almost 30 feet (9 meters) in the last 100 years.

Underground Limestone Cavern Formed by Water

Courtesy of www.photos.com

Text adapted from *Planet Under Pressure (BBC)*

Tour Stop 5: Dams

In the last century, dams became a popular way of creating power. Hydroelectric power is cheaper and cleaner than electricity produced by fossil fuels. In addition, water is considered a renewable resource by many people because precipitation always falls. However, dams can create as many problems as they solve.

In Turkey, many dams have been built on the Tigris and Euphrates rivers. Turkey has worked hard in the past fifty years to increase its water supply and make hydroelectricity available to its citizens. Compared to many of its neighbors, Turkey has immense water supplies without the dams. Therefore, Turkey's dam construction has been protested by many countries downriver, such as Syria and Iraq. These countries rely on the Tigris and Euphrates rivers as their major sources of water. Turkey plans to build more dams, but it will have to negotiate with its neighbors to make these plans happen peacefully.

China is another country that has used dams to control its water. China faces problems with flooding in the south and drought in the north. The best solution seemed to be damming up the major rivers that flow through both areas. This reduced flooding in the south and provided water for the parched north. The Three Gorges Dam is one such project currently underway in China. However, all three rivers affected by this project are severely polluted. The dams do nothing to reduce pollution.

Center Hill Dam, Tennessee

Courtesy of www.photos.com

Text adapted from *Planet Under Pressure (BBC)*

Tour Stop 6: Irrigation

Many rivers are used for irrigation of crops. Water is diverted from these rivers and lakes to water crops in areas where there is not enough precipitation. As the world's population increases, so does the need for food. Both crops and animals depend on water to survive. Animals require roughly five times the amount of water that plant crops do, so countries where meat is a main food face a greater need for more water.

The Nile River is the main source of water for the entire country of Egypt. It is a source of conflict among the ten countries through which it flows. Because Egypt has almost no other source of water, the Egyptian government strongly opposes any projects upriver that would decrease its access to the river and has said in the past that it would use force if needed. However, other countries along the river—such as Ethiopia and Tanzania—also face water shortages and would like to use water from the Nile to address their needs. Both countries have plans to divert water from the Nile for drinking and crop irrigation.

Between the Tigris and Euphrates rivers in Iraq lies one of the world's largest wetland systems. However, almost 90% of these marshes have dried up due to irrigation and canal systems put in place over the last 20 years. In addition, Turkish dams upriver have significantly reduced the volume of water flowing into the area. Recent efforts by local people to restore the wetlands have had mixed results, as much of the water is contaminated.

Rice Paddy in Asia

Courtesy of www.photos.com

Text adapted from *Planet Under Pressure (BBC)*

Tour Stop 7: Shrinking Lakes and Seas

Lake Chad in Africa and the Aral Sea in Central Asia are two inland bodies of water facing massive depletion. Lake Chad has shrunk over 90% in the last 40 years. The Aral Sea was the world's fourth largest lake 35 years ago. It is now the world's eighth largest lake.

In the case of Lake Chad, changes in local weather patterns are the main cause of its evaporation. Monsoons that used to blow over the lake yearly, bringing essential rain, have shrunk in recent years. They no longer bring enough rain to replenish the lake. Overgrazing and irrigation have contributed to the problem, making water shortages common for the nine million people who live around the lake.

The Aral Sea suffered massive depletion under Soviet control. The two rivers that feed into the sea were diverted for irrigation of cotton crops. Because Central Asia is semi-arid, these crops required a lot of water. As a result, the Aral Sea is not only shrinking, it is becoming poisonous. Less water flowing into the sea has caused the salinity (saltiness) of the sea to increase, killing plants and animals that live in it.

A Stranded Boat in a Shrinking Lake

Courtesy of www.photos.com

Text adapted from *Planet Under Pressure* (BBC)

World Water Tour

Directions: Begin your tour at any of the stations around the room. At each stop, read the information and look at the picture. Then, record your answers to the corresponding questions on this sheet.

Tour Stop 1: The Earth's Water Supply

1. How much of Earth's fresh water is available for human use?

   _____

2. Do you think water is a renewable resource? Why or why not?

   _____

   _____

   _____

Tour Stop 2: Ancient Civilizations and Water

1. How long ago did people start to settle near water sources?

   _____

2. How do you think irrigation contributed to the growth of cities?

   _____

   _____

   _____

Tour Stop 3: Water and Population

1. Roughly how many people in the world struggle to get enough water?

   _____

2. Which do you think is a bigger threat—water pollution or the growth of agriculture? Why?

   _____

   _____

   _____

World Water Tour *(cont.)*

Tour Stop 4: Aquifer Depletion

1. What is an aquifer?

_____

2. What do you think might be some alternatives to using fossil water?

_____

_____

Tour Stop 5: Dams

1. Why do countries develop hydroelectric power?

_____

2. Describe a country that might be likely to develop hydroelectricity.

_____

_____

Tour Stop 6: Irrigation

1. What is irrigation?

_____

2. Do you think countries upriver have an obligation to consider the welfare of the countries downriver? Why or why not?

_____

_____

Tour Stop 7: Shrinking Lakes and Seas

1. What causes lakes and seas to shrink?

_____

2. What steps might farmers and ranchers take to slow the shrinking of the Aral Sea and Lake Chad?

_____

_____

_____

News Report Roles Sheet

Reporter: person who delivers the information to the camera

This person may use notes to present the information or may have it memorized. The reporter will also conduct an interview with one or two people who live in an area without adequate water. The reporter must have good eye contact and a firm, clear voice. There may be more than one reporter.

Interviewee: person who lives in an area without adequate water supplies

This person will be interviewed by the reporter and should not use notes. It is the job of the interviewee to make people want to help his or her area of the world, so it's important for this person to be prepared and animated when he or she is interviewed. There may be more than one interviewee.

Anchor: the main news person

He or she stays at the news desk and introduces the reporter. His or her main job is to transition smoothly from one reporter to another. The anchor can also use notes but must maintain good eye contact. There can only be one anchor, and a group may opt not to use an anchor at all.

Camera person (if videotaping): person who operates the camera, keeping it smooth and focused at all times

The camera person must follow the action in the report, changing from anchor to reporter to interviewee and back. It is important for this person to have a very steady hand and a good eye for composition (how things look together). The teacher may play the role of the camera person.

Director: person who leads all of the "actors" through the news report.

In a large group (six or more people) it may be helpful to have a director to take the lead. Everyone must follow the director's instructions, so the director must be able to communicate quickly and effectively.

Water Research Questions

Directions: Answer the following questions. Your news report should be based on your answers. Use more paper, as necessary, to complete your answers.

1. What issue is your group researching?

2. What areas of the world does your issue affect?

3. Will you use a map to show your audience these areas? If so, which map?

4. What are the causes of your issue?

5. What are the effects of your issue?

6. What are the two (or more) sides of your issue?

7. Describe your issue from each side.

   • Side 1:

   • Side 2:

   • Side 3:

8. Have there been any attempts to compromise?

World Water Tour Key

Directions: Begin your tour at any of the stations around the room. At each stop, read the information and look at the picture. Then, record your answers to the corresponding questions on this sheet.

Tour Stop 1: The Earth's Water Supply

1. How much of Earth's fresh water is available for human use?
   (less than 1%)

2. Do you think water is a renewable resource? Why or why not?
   (Answers will vary but should include the fact that there is a finite amount of water in the world.)

Tour Stop 2: Ancient Civilizations and Water

1. How long ago did people start to settle near water sources?
   (about 12,000 years ago)

2. How do you think irrigation contributed to the growth of cities?
   (Answers will vary but should include the fact that irrigation led to larger crops which could feed more people.)

Tour Stop 3: Water and Population

1. Roughly how many people in the world struggle to get enough water?
   (approximately 2 billion, which includes whole populations that live in countries with water issues)

2. Which do you think is a bigger threat—water pollution or the growth of agriculture? Why? *(Answers will vary but should be supported by evidence.)*

World Water Tour Key *(cont.)*

Tour Stop 4: Aquifer Depletion

1. What is an aquifer? *(an underground reservoir of fossil [ancient] water)*

2. What do you think might be some alternatives to using fossil water? *(Answers will vary but may include irrigation, buying water from other countries, using virtual water [plants that hold water], desalination of sea water, etc.)*

Tour Stop 5: Dams

1. Why do countries develop hydroelectric power? *(It is cheaper and cleaner than power from fossil fuels. Water is also considered a renewable resource, unlike fossil fuels.)*

2. Describe a country that might be likely to develop hydroelectricity. *(a developed country because dams are expensive to build, with at least one big river and space for a reservoir)*

Tour Stop 6: Irrigation

1. What is irrigation? *(diverting water from rivers, lakes, or seas to water crops in areas without enough annual precipitation to support those crops)*

2. Do you think countries upriver have an obligation to the countries downriver? Why or why not? *(Answers will vary but should be supported by evidence.)*

Tour Stop 7: Shrinking Lakes and Seas

1. What causes lakes and seas to shrink? *(climate change, irrigation, and overgrazing)*

2. What steps might farmers and ranchers take to slow the shrinking of the Aral Sea and Lake Chad? *(Answers will vary but may include changing to crops or animals that require less water, building basins to catch rainwater to use, etc.)*

Culture Quest

Overview

In this activity, students explore the factors that determine people's cultural identities. Students compare and contrast languages and religions, then create and perform monologues of characters from other cultures.

The answer key for student reproducibles is located at the end of the lesson. It is helpful for the teacher to examine such keys before beginning the lesson or distributing any reproducibles to the class. This type of advance inspection will (1) improve teacher understanding and presentation, (2) prepare the teacher for possible alternative student responses, (3) help with classroom time management, and (4) result in optimum focus and effectiveness for the activity.

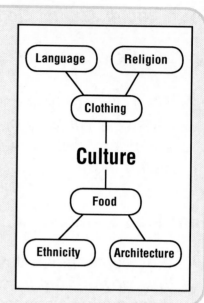

Objective

- Students will understand the nature and complexity of Earth's cultural mosaics.

Central Question

Does culture cause more unity or more division?

Materials

You will need to prepare and/or provide the following:

- Internet websites or other research resources
- *Friend Cards* (one per student), page 120
- *Cultural Identity Notes* (one per student), page 121
- overhead transparency of *Cultural Identity Notes*
- *World Religions Handout* (one per student), page 122

- overhead transparency of *World Religions Handout*
- *Monologue Research* (one per student), page 123
- *Monologue Practice Assessment* (cut apart; one per student), page 124

Answer Keys

Culture Quest *(cont.)*

Directions

Day One

1. As your students enter your room, give each one a *Friend Card.*

2. Ask for volunteers to read the words on their cards out loud. After several have read their cards, ask students to think about what each card means.

3. Tell students the cards all say *friend* or *friends* in different languages. (Because of differences among languages, some of the pronunciations are approximate.)

4. There are approximately 6,809 languages in the world. Ask your students, "In an increasingly interconnected world, what problems might this cause?"

5. Ask students to circulate around the room, looking for people with words for *friend* that are similar to theirs. Have them group themselves according to any similarities that they note. Ask the following questions:

   • What are the similarities among your languages?

   • How might geography relate to the similarities and differences?

   • Why are some groups larger than others?

6. Pass out copies of *Cultural Identity Notes.* Fill in the information as a class (using the answers on page 126 as reference), and answer of your students' questions.

Day Two

1. Distribute copies of the *World Religions Handout.*

2. Give your students about ten minutes to connect religions by their similarities and to highlight differences between religions.

3. Ask your students the following questions:

   • Are there more similarities or more differences among these religions?

   • How might having different religions in a region create conflict? Unity?

4. *Arts Integration:* A monologue is a speech given by one person, describing his or her thoughts, feelings, and actions. Your students will create and perform monologues depicting fictional people from other cultures.

5. Assign each student a country or allow students to choose their own.

6. Pass out copies of *Monologue Research.*

7. Give your students ample time to research their characters, using the Internet or other research resources.

8. Suggest to your students that they create simple costumes for their characters, to add realism to their performances.

Day Three

1. Place students into small groups of three or four.

2. Distribute copies of the *Monologue Practice Assessment.*

3. Tell students they will practice their monologues in small groups. The other members of the groups will assess the performances and offer suggestions for improvement. When students are ready, have them do their monologues for the whole class. You may wish to videotape the performances.

Friend Cards

Vriende (vreen da)	Nazdardru (naz dar droo)
Amis (ah mee)	Sokulgan (so kool gan)
Freunde (froyn da)	Filoi (fee loy)
Amici (ah mee chee)	Pagkakaibigan (pag ka kai bee gan)
Venner (vay ner)	Kawan (kah wan)
Bekendte (bey kend ta)	Mitra (mee tra)
Cairde (kair da)	Miuchi (mee oo chee)
Amigos (ah mee goes)	Chou (choo)
Sadiq (sa deek)	Vriendin (vreen den)
Druga (droo ga)	Rafiki (rah fee kee)
Priatelstvo (pree a tell stva)	Umngane (oom gahn)
Prieten (pree ay ten)	Gwaa de (gwah day)

Cultural Identity Notes

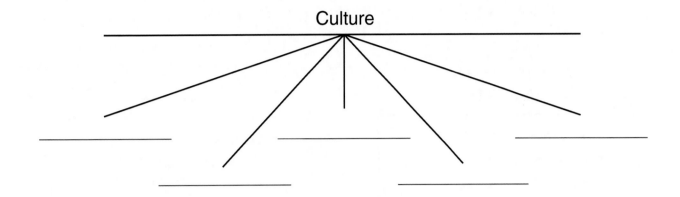

Culture

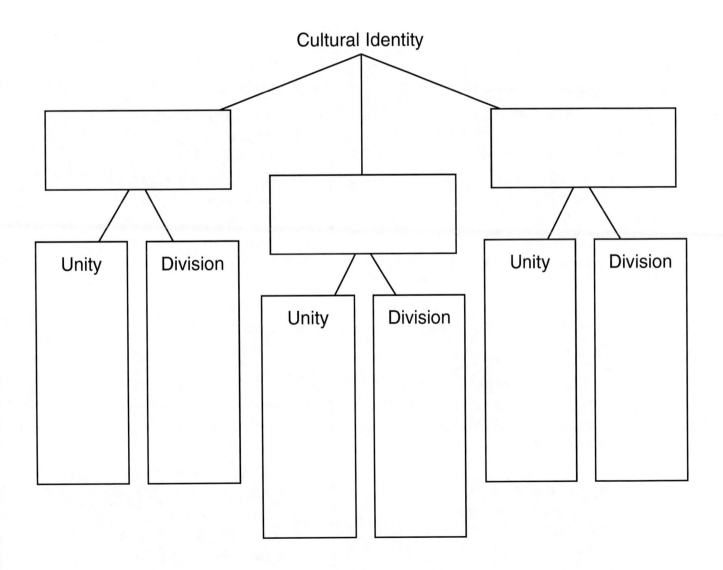

Cultural Identity

Unity   Division

Unity   Division

Unity   Division

World Religions Handout

Create lines connecting religions that share a feature in common. Use your highlighter or a crayon to highlight features that are unique to a religion.

Judaism

- Jerusalem is a holy site.
- *Torah* is holy book.
- Abraham started it around 2000 B.C.
- Passover, Rosh Hashanah, Yom Kippur are holy days.

Hinduism

- Ganges River is holy site.
- *Bhagavad Gita* and *The Vedas* are holy books.
- Began around 2000 B.C.
- Diwali and Holi are holy days.

Buddhism

- Bodhi trees are holy.
- *Pali Canon* is holy book.
- Began 530 B.C.
- Buddha Day is a celebration.
- It came from Hinduism.

Confucianism

- Temples are holy sites.
- *The Analects* is holy book.
- Began around 530 B.C.
- Teacher's Day is a celebration.

Christianity

- Jerusalem and Bethlehem are holy sites.
- *Bible* is holy book.
- Began around A.D. 30.
- Christmas and Easter are holy days.
- It came from Judaism.

Islam

- Mecca, Medina, and Jerusalem are holy sites.
- *Qur'an* is holy book.
- Began around A.D. 600.
- Ramadan, Id al-Fitr, and Id al-Adha are holy days.
- It came from Judaism.

Monologue Research

Directions: A monologue is a form of theatrical story telling. Your monologue will be a speech given in the first person ("I"), telling the story of the cultural character you create. You may use simple props, such as clothing, to create a more realistic experience for you and your audience. In order to write your monologue, you must first complete research to answer the following questions. Write your answers on other sheets paper.

1. What country will you research?

2. What is your character's first name?

3. What language(s) does your character speak?

4. How would your character say "hello"?

5. What religion would your character practice?

6. What are one or two major beliefs of that religion?

7. How does your character's religion determine his or her perception of the world?

8. What is your character's ethnicity?

9. Is this ethnicity similar to any other ethnicities? Which ones?

10. What foods might your character eat regularly? Are there any particular rules about eating that your character would follow?

11. What art forms might your character create? Describe them or create a sample to display during your monologue.

12. Are there any articles of clothing that your character would or would not wear? What are they?

13. Describe your character's home. Are there any special rooms or special furnishings? What are their purposes?

Now you are ready to write your monologue. Remember to use the first person ("I") and to make your character appealing to your audience. Your character should be about the same age as you.

Monologue Practice Assessment

Name of performer: _____   Name of character: _____

Eye Contact	needs work	so-so	good	outstanding
Clarity of Voice	needs work	so-so	good	outstanding
Gestures	needs work	so-so	good	outstanding
Props	needs work	so-so	good	outstanding
Completeness of Information	needs work	so-so	good	outstanding
Staying In Character	needs work	so-so	good	outstanding
Notes			

Name of performer: _____   Name of character: _____

Eye Contact	needs work	so-so	good	outstanding
Clarity of Voice	needs work	so-so	good	outstanding
Gestures	needs work	so-so	good	outstanding
Props	needs work	so-so	good	outstanding
Completeness of Information	needs work	so-so	good	outstanding
Staying In Character	needs work	so-so	good	outstanding
Notes			

Friend Cards Key

Vriende (vreen da) *Dutch*	Nazdardru (naz dar droo) *Czech*
Amis (ah-mee) *French*	Sokulgan (so kool gan) *Turkish*
Freunde (froyn da) *German*	Filoi (fee loy) *Greek*
Amici (ah mee chee) *Italian*	Pagkakaibigan (pag ka kai bee gan) *Tagalog*
Venner (vay ner) *Norwegian*	Kawan (kah wan) *Malay*
Bekendte (bey kend ta) *Danish*	Mitra (mee tra) *Hindi*
Cairde (kair da) *Irish Gaelic*	Miuchi (mee oo chee) *Japanese*
Amigos (ah mee goes) *Spanish*	Chou (choo) *Chinese*
Sadiq (sa deek) *Arabic*	Vriendin (vreen den) *Afrikaans*
Druga (droo ga) *Russian*	Rafiki (rah fee kee) *Swahili*
Priatelstvo (pree a tell stva) *Bulgarian*	Umngane (oom gahn) *Zulu*
Prieten (pree ay ten) *Romanian*	Gwaa de (gwah day) *Amharic*

Cultural Identity Notes Key

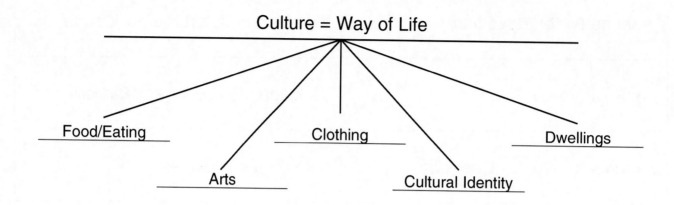

Culture = Way of Life

Food/Eating   Clothing   Dwellings

Arts   Cultural Identity

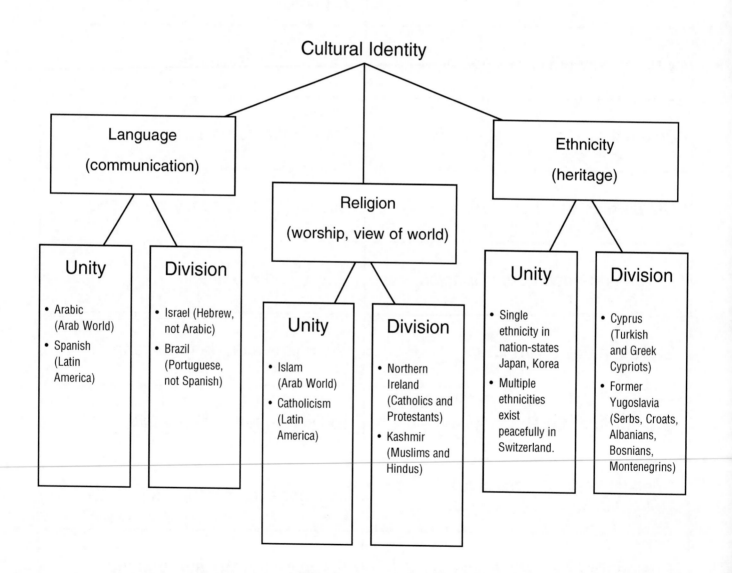

Cultural Identity

Language
(communication)

Ethnicity
(heritage)

Religion
(worship, view of world)

Unity
- Arabic (Arab World)
- Spanish (Latin America)

Division
- Israel (Hebrew, not Arabic)
- Brazil (Portuguese, not Spanish)

Unity
- Islam (Arab World)
- Catholicism (Latin America)

Division
- Northern Ireland (Catholics and Protestants)
- Kashmir (Muslims and Hindus)

Unity
- Single ethnicity in nation-states Japan, Korea
- Multiple ethnicities exist peacefully in Switzerland.

Division
- Cyprus (Turkish and Greek Cypriots)
- Former Yugoslavia (Serbs, Croats, Albanians, Bosnians, Montenegrins)

World Religions Handout Key

Note: Students may make more connections than those shown below, which should lead to a discussion of "common features" and "unique features."

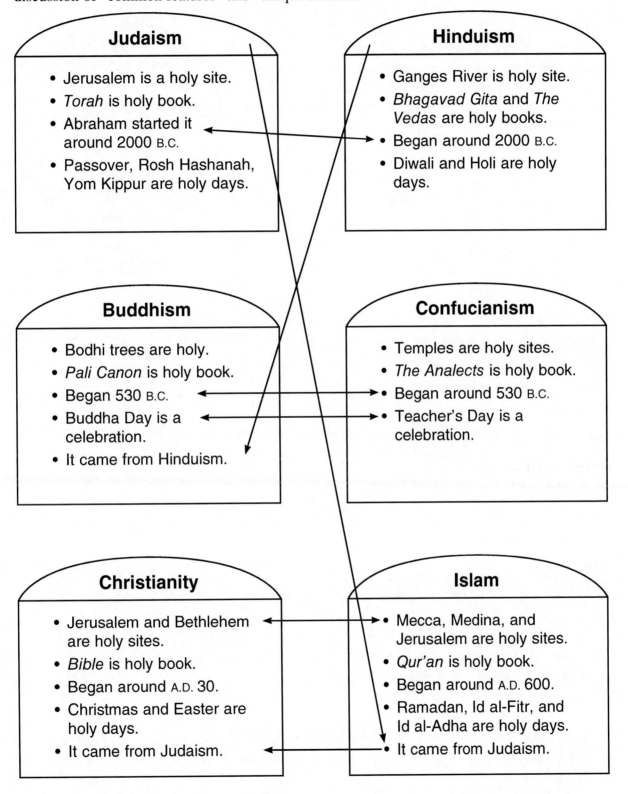

Judaism

- Jerusalem is a holy site.
- *Torah* is holy book.
- Abraham started it around 2000 B.C.
- Passover, Rosh Hashanah, Yom Kippur are holy days.

Hinduism

- Ganges River is holy site.
- *Bhagavad Gita* and *The Vedas* are holy books.
- Began around 2000 B.C.
- Diwali and Holi are holy days.

Buddhism

- Bodhi trees are holy.
- *Pali Canon* is holy book.
- Began 530 B.C.
- Buddha Day is a celebration.
- It came from Hinduism.

Confucianism

- Temples are holy sites.
- *The Analects* is holy book.
- Began around 530 B.C.
- Teacher's Day is a celebration.

Christianity

- Jerusalem and Bethlehem are holy sites.
- *Bible* is holy book.
- Began around A.D. 30.
- Christmas and Easter are holy days.
- It came from Judaism.

Islam

- Mecca, Medina, and Jerusalem are holy sites.
- *Qur'an* is holy book.
- Began around A.D. 600.
- Ramadan, Id al-Fitr, and Id al-Adha are holy days.
- It came from Judaism.

Money Makes the World Go 'Round

Overview

In this activity, students analyze the connections between physical geography and the ways that people make money. They research physical and economic characteristics of a country, and engage in an auction to draw conclusions about geography and economics.

Courtesy of www.clipart.com

Objective

- Students will understand the patterns and networks of economic interdependence on Earth's surface.

Central Question

How does physical geography affect economics?

Materials

You will need to prepare and/or provide the following:

- research resources (Internet, encyclopedias, atlases, almanacs, etc.)
- *Country Research Notes* (one per student), page 132
- *Country Markers* (cut apart; one per group), page 133
- overhead transparency of *PCI Discussion Questions*, page 134
- *Moolah*, page 135
- incentives for the auction (See page 176 for *Suggested Incentives*.)
- *Economics Discussion Questions* (one per student), page 136
- overhead transparency of *Political Cartoon*, page 137
- *Political Cartoon Directions* (one per student), page 138

Money Makes the World Go 'Round *(cont.)*

Directions

Day One

1. Select a region that you want your students to study.

2. *Optional:* Before you start this activity, you may wish to arrange your room to represent the region you are studying to help your students visualize the area. You can use construction cones or "Wet Floor" signs to represent mountains, blue construction paper for rivers, etc.

3. Arrange your students in groups of three to five. Assign each group a country in the region you are studying.

4. Give each student a copy of *Country Research Notes*, and allow them about 20 minutes to complete their research on their assigned countries.

5. Pass out the country markers (one per group) and have your students fill in the information.

6. One student from each group should come to the front of the room with the group's marker. These students should arrange themselves in order from the highest to the lowest per capita income (PCI).

7. Display the *PCI Discussion Questions* on the overhead and lead a class discussion on how and why natural resources are important to a country's economy.

8. For homework, have your students bring in small items from home for the auction, based on their country's PCI. (**Note:** Please make sure your students have permission to bring in household items.) Each team can bring one item to sell for every $500 PCI their country has. Teams can, however, bring in extra items to auction if they relate directly to one of their country's main exports. For example, if lumber and paper products are major exports, pencils and paper products would be permitted in the auction, in addition to the items related to PCI.

Day Two

1. Before class, cut out enough *Moolah* for the class auction. For every $100 PCI, each team is given $1.00 in *Moolah* (round the PCI to the nearest $100).

2. Have the teams auction off their items in random order. You may wish to add an item-viewing period before the auction begins to help the teams decide how to spend their *Moolah*. However, do not let your students know about your incentive items.

3. When all the teams are finished buying and selling, auction off your incentives. These items should be auctioned to the highest bidders. Only the teams that used their economic resources wisely will be able to purchase these items. You may wish to bring in enough incentives to hand out extras to people who couldn't participate in the auction.

4. At the end of class (or for homework), ask each student to write down three or four observations about the auction and how it might tie into economics.

Money Makes the World Go 'Round *(cont.)*

Directions *(cont.)*

Day Three

1. Ask for volunteers to share their observations from the homework. Use these observations to introduce the idea that natural sources have an impact on economics.

2. Divide your students into mixed-ability groups of three or four.

3. Give each student a copy of the *Economics Discussion Questions*. Allow the groups to discuss possible answers to each question. Their answers should be oral at this point. Monitor the groups to make sure that they are staying on topic.

4. Create a fish bowl by placing five or six chairs in a circle in the center of the room. Place the remaining chairs in a circle around the center circle.

5. Explain to your students that they will be participating in a Socratic Seminar. The students in the center circle will discuss their answers to the *Economic Discussion Questions* as a group. The students in the outer circle will summarize the center group's discussion. Everyone will have the opportunity to be in the center circle.

6. Explain the rules of Socratic Seminar to your students:

   - One student speaks at a time.
   - Wait for a break in the discussion to change topics.
   - It's okay to disagree with each other, but do it respectfully.
   - No name calling, teasing, or other insults.
   - If you are in the center circle, you are expected to contribute to the conversation.
   - You must be in the center circle to participate.

7. Ask for volunteers to be in the center circle. Leave one chair in the center unoccupied. This is the "hot seat." Any student in the outer circle may take the "hot seat" if he or she wants to contribute to the discussion. Unless they are in the "hot seat," students in the outer circle cannot contribute to the discussion.

8. Your job is to moderate the discussion. Start by asking one of the questions from *Economics Discussion Questions*. Listen to your students' responses, and make sure that the students in the outer circle are listening and summarizing. Also, make sure no one from the outer circle is monopolizing the "hot seat." If you want to steer your students in a particular direction, or you think they are missing a point, take the "hot seat" yourself and add your question and/or comment.

9. You can switch center circle students after each question or less frequently, depending on the size of your class and your students' abilities to participate.

Money Makes the World Go 'Round *(cont.)*

Directions *(cont.)*

Day Three *(cont.)*

10. If you wish to grade this activity, you can collect the summaries from your students at the end of the class. You can also grade students' participation in the center circle, using a simple point scale:

    - 3 points: comment shows insight as well as references the research or the auction
    - 2 points: comment references research or auction
    - 1 points: comment offers opinion but no support
    - 0 points: comment is simply a reiteration of another student's point
    - -1 point: comment is off the topic or inappropriate

Day Four

1. *Arts Integration:* Display the overhead of the *Political Cartoon* "Juice." Explain to your students that political cartoons are usually single-scene drawings that make a comment on an issue. This image, from "The Best of Latin America," is making the point that natural resources are stretched to their limit and will run out sooner rather than later.

2. Distribute copies of *Political Cartoon Directions*, and go through the discussion questions with your students.

3. Have your students create their own political cartoons. You may wish to have them work in groups, pairs, or individually. You may find it helpful to coordinate this activity with your school's art teacher.

Country Research Notes

- Name of country: _____
- Physical features of your country:

    River(s) _____

    Mountains _____

    Deserts _____

    Bodies of water (lakes, oceans, seas, etc.) _____

    Other _____

- Natural Resources: _____

    _____

- Exports: _____

    _____

- How do the exports relate to the natural resources and physical features of your country? _____

    _____

- Name of country: _____
- Physical features of your country:

    River(s) _____

    Mountains _____

    Deserts _____

    Bodies of water (lakes, oceans, seas, etc.) _____

    Other _____

- Natural Resources: _____

    _____

- Exports: _____

    _____

- How do the exports relate to the natural resources and physical features of your country? _____

    _____

Country Markers

Country: _____

PCI: _____

Country: _____

PCI: _____

Country: _____

PCI: _____

Country: _____

PCI: _____

PCI Discussion Questions

1. Which country has the highest PCI? The lowest?

2. What do the countries with the highest PCIs export? How might this affect their PCIs?

3. What do the countries with the lowest PCIs export? How might this affect their PCIs?

4. Do the three countries with the highest PCIs share a common export or natural resource? What is it?

5. Do the three countries with the lowest PCIs share a common export or natural resource? What is it?

6. How do each country's physical features affect its PCI? Are there any physical features that might increase or hinder trade?

You will experience the unbalanced nature of international trade during the next day's auction!

Moolah

Economics Discussion Questions

1. Was your team able to purchase everything you wanted?

2. How does the auction from yesterday apply to countries in real life?

3. List at least two specific events that occurred during the auction, and tell what they might represent in global trade.

4. How well did the countries with low PCIs compete with their wealthier neighbors?

5. How can a nation with limited natural resources compete with neighboring countries that have more resources?

6. Can a nation with few natural resources use other resources to make it richer?

Political Cartoon

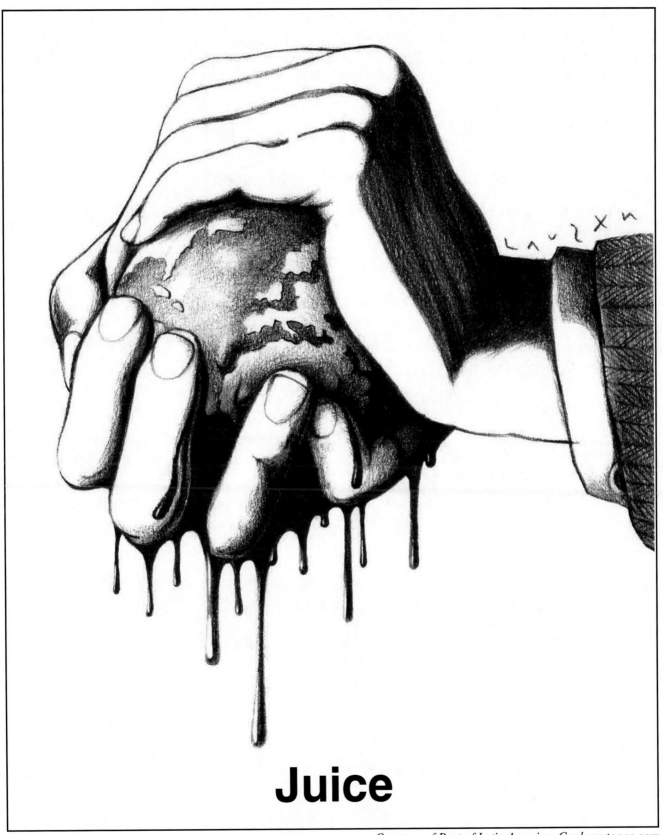

Juice

Courtesy of Best of Latin America, Caglecartoons.com

Political Cartoon Directions

A political cartoon is a drawing that makes a comment on a current issue. Political cartoons usually consist of one or two frames (drawings) and can be in color or black and white. On page 137 is a cartoon called "Juice" from *The Best of Latin America*.

Directions: As you examine the political cartoon on page 137, answer the following discussion questions.

- What is the event or issue that inspired the cartoon?

- What background knowledge do you need in order to understand the message?

- Are there any real people in the cartoon?

- Did the artist use caricatures? Are there symbols in the cartoon?

- What is the cartoonist's opinion about the topic portrayed?

- Does the caption help you understand the message?

- Do you agree or disagree with the cartoonist's opinion? Why?

Now, create your own political cartoon, answering the question: "How does physical geography affect economics?" Your cartoon can be in color or black and white and should include a caption. Use the discussion questions above and the questions below to help guide your work.

1. What point do you want to make about the ties between physical geography and economics?

2. What symbols can you use to illustrate your point?

3. What might your caption say to help explain your cartoon?

Who's in Charge?

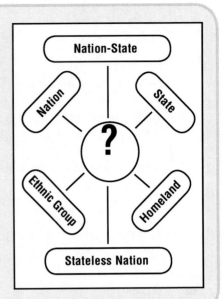

Overview

In this activity, students investigate the main types of government and compare how power is distributed in each system by experiencing life under each type of system. Students then create mobiles representing the different types of government.

The answer key for student reproducibles is located at the end of the lesson. It is helpful for the teacher to examine such keys before beginning the lesson or distributing any reproducibles to the class. This type of advance inspection will (1) improve teacher understanding and presentation, (2) prepare the teacher for possible alternative student responses, (3) help with classroom time management, and (4) result in optimum focus and effectiveness for the activity.

Objective

- Students will understand the forces of cooperation and conflict that shape the divisions of Earth's surface.

Central Question

How does the distribution of power influence people's lives?

Materials

You will need to prepare and/or provide the following:

- *Nation and State Notes* (one per student), page 142
- overhead transparency of *Nation and State Notes*
- *Political Readings* (one set per student), pages 143–146
- *New Classroom Rules* (cut apart; one per student), page 147

- *Types of Government* (one per student), page 148
- overhead transparency of *Types of Government*
- paper clips
- drinking straws
- construction paper (or other heavy paper)
- scissors
- markers, crayons, etc.

Answer Keys

Nation and State Notes Key . . . . .page 149

Types of Government Key . . . . .page 150

Who's in Charge? *(cont.)*

Directions

Day One

1. Distribute copies of *Nation and State Notes.*

2. Lead a class discussion on nations and states, using the overhead and answer key on page 149 to fill in the notes as you go.

3. Answer students' questions to make sure they understand the differences among the different nations and states.

4. Distribute copies of the *Political Readings.* As a class, read the section on Cyprus. Go over the answers to the questions together. Have your students finish the rest of the readings and questions on their own.

Day Two

1. Review the terms *state, nation, nation-state,* and *stateless nation.* Then, go over the *Political Readings* answers.

2. Explain to your students that your classroom can be an example of political struggle. You make rules that you expect your students to follow. They may not agree with your rules. Do they have any recourse?

3. Announce that, despite any previous agreements on the rules, you have decided to implement new rules.

4. Distribute copies of the *New Classroom Rules* and the *Types of Government.*

5. Enforce the new rules as you fill in Section 1 of *Types of Government* handout. Dole out punishments as you see fit. There are no suggestions for punishments, so you can tailor the experience to your students.

6. After about five minutes, expect much protest. Still following the rules, elicit from students why they don't like these rules.

7. Select a small group of homogeneous students (three to five students). Ask them to move to the back of the room (or the hallway if necessary) to modify the rules. Use a homogeneous group to ensure an unequal balance of power. You may wish to point out to them that they now are sharing power with you and can make rules that favor themselves as well. Give them five to ten minutes to come up with amendments to your rules. Let them know that you will still have final say in the rules.

8. While this group is modifying your rules, discuss the importance of power with the rest of the class, using the following questions:
   - How did you feel under the new rules? Why?
   - How might your experience relate to the people of a stateless nation?
   - How might states with multiple nations deal with political struggles?

Who's in Charge? *(cont.)*

Directions *(cont.)*

Day Two *(cont.)*

9. Ask your small group to return to the class and share their rules. You may wish to review them first. Following the new group's rules, fill in Section 2 of *Types of Government*.

10. Expect more protests. Ask your students what they think would be a fair balance of power.

11. Finish Section 3 and Section 4 of *Types of Government*.

12. Break your class up into small groups to create a binding set of classroom rules. Limit each group to one rule that they feel is fair to everyone in the room, including you. If you do not wish to implement all of the new rules, write them on the board or overhead and have the class vote on which one or two they would like to live by.

Day Three

1. *Arts Integration:* Mobiles are kinetic art that rely on balance and movement to create their effect. Because they shift with air currents, mobiles are constantly changing and offer a unique blend of movement and visual imagery. Alexander Calder is credited with creating the art form of mobiles.

2. On heavy paper (construction paper works well), have your students create a symbol for each of the types of government that you discussed. They will need to create symbols for dictatorship, totalitarianism, absolute monarchy, stratocracy, ideological party, theocracy, democracy, direct democracy, representative democracy, and constitutional monarchy.

3. Tell your students to cut out their symbols and to write the name of the type of government on one side of each symbol. They should write who's in charge and an example on the other side.

4. Using the straws and the paper clips, challenge your students to create mobiles that balance the two major types of government: dictatorships on one side and democracies on the other. They can create several layers under each heading, and use the weight of the paper clips and the length of the straws to achieve balance.

5. Create a display of the mobiles. Putting them in a high-traffic area (such as a hallway) will take advantage of their kinetic aspect. You may wish to coordinate this project with your art teacher.

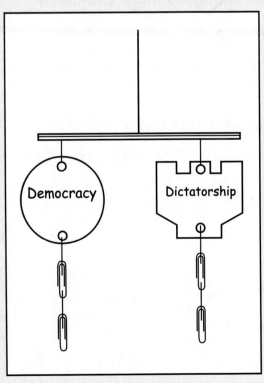

Nation and State Notes

Homelands

A _____ is a territory that an ethnic group considers part of its history and culture.

Some ethnic groups have lost their homelands. Some examples are the following:

American Indians (_____)   Aborigines (_____)
Indigenous tribes (_____)

Some ethnic groups have regained their homelands. Some examples are the following:

(_____) Canada   (_____) New Zealand

Sometimes, two or more ethnic groups claim the same homeland. An example is the following:

(_____)

Differences Between a Nation and a State

NATION = _____ (people with a shared culture) + _____ (territory)

STATE = _____ = _____ + _____ + _____ + _____ (complete independence, recognized by other states)

Some nations are stateless. These are cultures that want autonomy (_____ ____ _____), but do not have sovereignty (an internationally recognized government). Some examples are the following:

_____

_____

The leaders of these nations have power over their people, but little authority (official power). The central government has authority but little power.

Ethnicity and Statehood

Some states have dozens of nations and homelands within their boundaries. Some examples are the following:

Nigeria (_____ + ethnic groups, including _____, _____, _____, and _____)

_____ (1 state, 4 nations, including _____, _____ ____, _____, and _____)

Other states have only one nation within their boundaries. These are called _____ _____. The homeland matches the state's political borders. Some examples are the following:

_____   _____   _____

Political Readings: Cyprus

There are two main cultural groups living in Cyprus: the Greek Cypriots and the Turkish Cypriots. The Greek Cypriots have lived there for thousands of years, while the Turkish Cypriots arrived when the Ottoman Empire took over the island in the 1500s. Both ethnic groups claim Cyprus as their homeland. Many Greek Cypriots support wanting to unite with Greece. Many Turkish Cypriots, however, are against that idea. They would rather see the island divided into two separate nations. There are more Greek Cypriots than there are Turkish Cypriots. In 1960, Cyprus was declared an independent country with a government meant to protect the rights of the Turkish minority. However, partly because of the elaborate power sharing system, the government soon fell apart. In 1974, Turkey attacked Cyprus and took over the northern part of the island. The Turkish government claimed that it was protecting the Turkish Cypriots from Greek rule. In 1983, northern Cyprus declared its independence from the Republic of Cyprus. However, Turkey is the only country that recognizes this nation.

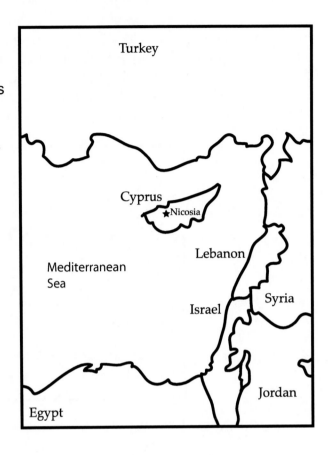

1. Summarize the reading (two sentences maximum).

_____

_____

2. How would you describe Northern Cyprus—nation? state? nation-state? stateless nation? Give reasons for your description.

_____

_____

_____

_____

_____

Political Readings: Spain

The Basque Provinces make up a small portion of the border between France and Spain. In Spain, the Basque territory is autonomous (has local control) but not independent. It is still part of Spain. This has led to violence between Basque groups who want complete sovereignty and the Spanish government. One Basque group, ETA, uses terrorist tactics to advance its political goals. Spain has responded by placing limits on Basque autonomy. For example, Spain has closed the major Basque newspaper, and has outlawed certain political parties.

1. Summarize the reading (two sentences maximum).

_____

_____

_____

2. How would you describe the Basque country—nation? state? nation-state? stateless nation? Give reasons for your description.

_____

_____

_____

_____

_____

Political Readings: Palestine

Both Palestinians and Israelis claim that the area between the Mediterranean Sea and Jordan is their homeland. The Jewish people originated in this area but were forced out thousands of years ago. The Arabs who moved into the area during their exile became known as Palestinians. In the late 1800s, Jewish people began to buy land in the area and establish farms. These local Jewish farmers, as well as other national and international groups, wanted to create a Jewish homeland. The United Nations tried for many years to create a plan for the two groups to share the land, but many Palestinians did not want to share it. The State of Israel was created in 1948. This angered many of the Palestinians who lived in the area, as well as Israel's neighboring Arab countries. Israel was attacked over the next several years by its Arab neighbors. As a result of these attacks, Israel annexed more land, including parts that were to be under Palestinian control. Israel retained control of these lands until recently, when they reverted back to Palestinian control.

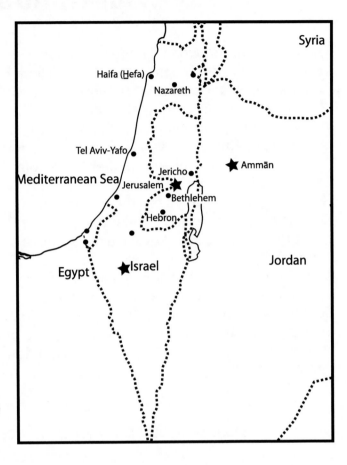

1. Summarize the reading (two sentences maximum).

_____

_____

_____

2. How would you describe Palestine—nation? state? nation-state? stateless nation? Give reasons for your description.

_____

_____

_____

_____

Political Readings: Kurdistan

The Kurds are the world's largest stateless minority. There are approximately 25 million Kurds living in a region between the countries of Turkey, Syria, Iraq, Iran, and Armenia. The largest Kurdish populations are found in Iraq and Turkey. Kurdistan was part of the Ottoman Empire, and when it broke up after World War I, the Kurds were promised independence. However, Turkey fought to keep its part of Kurdistan, and they won. Other surrounding countries supported Turkey's claim, because it meant they could keep their sections as well. The Kurds have been fighting for over 90 years for their independence. In Iraq and Turkey, Kurds have been culturally oppressed for many years. In 1988, Iraqi troops killed thousands of Kurds and destroyed hundreds of Kurdish villages. Turkey outlawed Kurdish schools where Kurdish traditions and language were taught. The Kurds' status in the region remains uncertain.

1. Summarize the reading (two sentences maximum).

   _____

   _____

   _____

   _____

2. How would you describe Kurdistan—nation? state? nation-state? stateless nation? Give reasons for your description.

   _____

   _____

   _____

   _____

New Classroom Rules

1. Students will arrive at class on time and prepared to work.

2. Students will address the teacher as "Your Majesty."

3. All work must be "A" quality, or it will not be accepted.

4. The teach can make up new rules at any time.

5. All work will be done to the best of the student's ability.

6. Students will raise their hands and wait to be called on.

7. Students will accept responsibility for their actions, good or bad.

8. Students are expected to shower the teacher with gifts on a weekly basis.

9. No students will leave the classroom for any reason.

10. The teacher is responsible for reminding the students of these rules.

1. Students will arrive at class on time and prepared to work.

2. Students will address the teacher as "Your Majesty."

3. All work must be "A" quality, or it will not be accepted.

4. The teach can make up new rules at any time.

5. All work will be done to the best of the student's ability.

6. Students will raise their hands and wait to be called on.

7. Students will accept responsibility for their actions, good or bad.

8. Students are expected to shower the teacher with gifts on a weekly basis.

9. No students will leave the classroom for any reason.

10. The teacher is responsible for reminding the students of these rules.

Types of Government

Who Has the Power?

Section 1: Politics = _____.

Political systems = how power is _____.

Absence of government = _____, meaning that no one is in charge.
For example, _____.

	Type of Government	Who's in Charge?	Example
Section 2:	AUTOCRACY • • •		
Section 3:	SPECIAL INTEREST • • •		
Section 4:	DEMOCRACY • • •		

Nation and State Notes Key

Homelands

A *(homeland)* is a territory that an ethnic group considers part of its history and culture.

Some ethnic groups have lost their homelands. Some examples are the following:

American Indians *(USA)*   Aborigines *(Australia)*   Indigenous tribes *(Brazil)*

Some ethnic groups have regained their homelands. Some examples are the following:

(Inuit) Canada   *(Maori)* New Zealand

Some ethnic groups claim the same homeland. An example is the following:

(Israelis and Palestinians)

Differences Between a Nation and a State

NATION = *Ethnic Group* (people with a shared culture) + *Homeland* (territory)

STATE = *(Country)* = *(people)* + *(land)* + *(government)* + *(sovereignty)* (complete independence, recognized by other states)

Some nations are stateless. These are cultures that want autonomy *(complete independence)* but do not have sovereignty (an internationally recognized government). Some examples are the following:

(Transdniester) Moldova, (Aceh) Indonesia, (Basque) Spain, (Corsica) France, (Tigre) Ethiopia, (Pathanistan) and (Baluchistan) Iran, Afghanistan, Pakistan, (Kalistan) India

The leaders of these nations have power over their people, but little authority (official power). The central government has authority but little power.

Ethnicity and Statehood

Some states have dozens of nations and homelands within their boundaries. Some examples are the following:

Nigeria *(300)* + ethnic groups, including *(Igbo, Hausa, Fulani,* and *Yoruba)*

(United Kingdom) 1 state, 4 nations, including *(England, Scotland, Wales,* and *Northern Ireland)*

Other states have only one nation within their boundaries. These are called *(nation-states)*. The homeland matches the state's political borders. Some examples are the following:

(Japan, Iceland, France)

Types of Government Key

Who Has the Power?

Section 1: Politics = *(power)*.

Political systems = how power is *(split among people and rulers)*.

Absence of government = *(anarchy)*, meaning that no one is in charge—for example, *(Somalia during the 1990s)*.

	Type of Government	Who's in Charge?	Example
Section 2:	AUTOCRACY • Dictatorship • Totalitarianism • Absolute monarchy	one person individual person extreme dictatorship royal family member	Cuba Nazi Germany Saudi Arabia
Section 3:	SPECIAL INTEREST • Stratocracy • Ideological party • Theocracy	small group of people soldiers politicians religious leaders	Libya China Iran
Section 4:	DEMOCRACY • Direct democracy • Representative • Constitutional monarchy	large group of people everyone elected officials elected officials + king or queen local government	United States The United Kingdom

Home Sweet Home

Overview

Students examine photographs on the Web of architecture from around the globe and analyze examples showing how architecture reflects the physical geography of a region. Then, they engage in a creative writing activity to synthesize their knowledge.

Courtesy of www.photos.com

The answer key for student reproducibles is located at the end of the lesson. It is helpful for the teacher to examine such keys before beginning the lesson or distributing any reproducibles to the class. This type of advance inspection will (1) improve teacher understanding and presentation, (2) prepare the teacher for possible alternative student responses, (3) help with classroom time management, and (4) result in optimum focus and effectiveness for the activity.

Objective

- Students will understand how physical systems affect human systems.

Central Question

How does architecture reflect the physical characteristics of a region?

Materials

You will need to prepare and/or provide the following:

- *Architecture Style Chart* (one per student), page 153
- overhead transparency of *Architecture Style Chart*
- *Venn Diagram* (one per student), page 154

Answer Key

Architecture Style Chart Key . . . . .page 155

Home Sweet Home *(cont.)*

Directions

1. Pass out the *Architecture Style Chart* to your students and display a copy on the overhead transparency. Tell your students that they will be conducting Internet research to find pictures of various architectural styles found around the world. Remind your students of proper "netiquette." See your school's information technology coordinator for more information on netiquette.

2. Direct your students to one of the search engines available on the Web:
   http://www.google.com
   http://www.yahoo.com
   http://www.askjeeves.com

   Once your students have opened one of the search engines, instruct them to click on the "Images" button before they enter their search criteria.

3. Give your students 20–25 minutes on the computer to research architectural styles, using the *Architecture Style Chart* to record their findings. If your time is limited, you may wish to assign groups of students to specific architectural styles.

4. Go over your students' research, entering information on the overhead as they direct you, and making sure that your students have accurate information.

5. When all of their information is complete, ask your students to choose one type of building from the chart. Tell them to imagine that they are visiting that place and to brainstorm comparisons between their chosen type of architecture and their own home. Your students should use the *Venn Diagram* to complete their comparisons.

6. *Arts Integration:* Ask your students to imagine that they are visiting the location they chose. They should then use their *Venn Diagrams* as preparation to write a letter to someone back home, explaining the similarities and differences between the two types of buildings and the reasons for them.

7. Remind your students of the conventions for writing an informal letter (include a salutation, body paragraph(s), a closing, and a signature). You may find it helpful to coordinate this activity with your English teacher.

Architecture Style Chart

Style	Description (Draw or Write)	Region	Adaptation to Geography
Houses on Stilts			
Chalets			
Thatched Roofs			
Floating Markets			
Open-Air Markets			
Windmills			

Venn Diagram

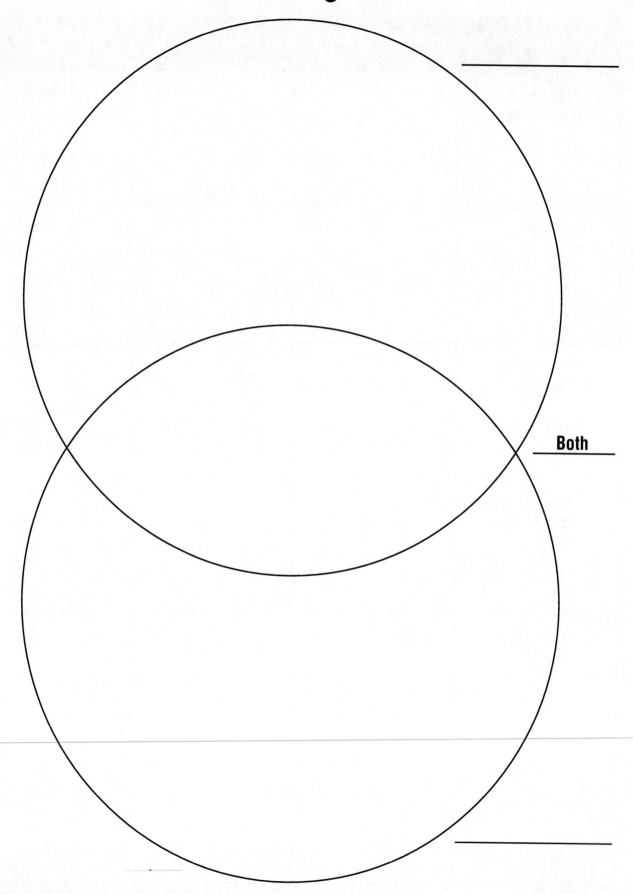

Both _____

Architecture Style Chart Key

Style	Description (Draw or Write)	Region	Adaptation to Geography
Houses on Stilts		*Pacific Islands, Southeastern United States*	*Area is subject to flooding and may have monsoons or wet season.*
Chalets		*Europe*	*Area has a lot of snow. Sloped roofs allow snow to slide off and also allow heat to stay lower in the house.*
Thatched Roofs		*Tropical islands*	*Palm trees dominate vegetation. Weather does not require insulation from cold.*
Floating Markets		*Southeast Asia*	*Waterways are more developed than roads. Area has hot/ warm weather most of the year.*
Open-Air Markets		*Africa*	*Area has hot/warm weather most of the year and little rain.*
Windmills		*Europe, Western United States*	*Areas have enough wind to provide energy. Mountains or hills may be nearby.*

Balancing Act

Overview

In small groups, students read about specific types of human-environment interaction (HEI). Then, students write and perform raps about the causes and effects of HEI.

Courtesy of www.clipart.com

The answer key for student reproducibles is located at the end of the lesson. It is helpful for the teacher to examine such keys before beginning the lesson or distributing any reproducibles to the class. This type of advance inspection will (1) improve teacher understanding and presentation, (2) prepare the teacher for possible alternative student responses, (3) help with classroom time management, and (4) result in optimum focus and effectiveness for the activity.

Objectives

- Students will understand how human actions modify the physical environment.
- Students will understand how physical systems affect human systems.

Central Question

Do the positive effects of HEI outweigh the negative effects? Why or why not?

Materials

You will need to prepare and/or provide the following:
- *HEI Notes* (one per student), pages 158–159
- overhead transparency of *HEI Notes*
- reading packet (one topic per group, either *Terracing, Desertification, Polders, Pollution,* or *Deforestation*), pages 160–164
- *Rap Directions* (one per group), page 165

Answer Key

Balancing Act *(cont.)*

Directions

Day One

1. Distribute a copy of the *HEI Notes* to each student. Explain to your students that they will be working in groups to become experts on one form of HEI (human-environment interaction).

2. Divide your students into groups of three or four. Give each group one set of readings. For example, if you have groups of four, the pollution group will need four copies of the *Pollution* handout, the terracing group will need four copies of the *Terracing* handout, and so on.

3. Each group must read the background material on its topic. Then, they should fill in the corresponding section of their notes.

4. As each group finishes their notes, check their answers for accuracy.

5. *Arts Integration:* Distribute copies of the *Rap Directions* to the group. Each group will create a rap explaining their topic. The rap should be four to six lines long and can use any type of rhyme scheme, including end rhyme, internal rhyme, alliteration, or free verse. You may wish to choose a song with which your students are familiar or you may want the groups to choose their own rhythms from songs that they know. You may also wish to allow the groups to create their own rhythms.

6. Give the groups time to create and rehearse their raps.

Day Two

1. When all of the groups have rehearsed and feel confident, each group performs its rap, and the rest of the class uses their performance to fill in the corresponding section of their notes. Or, after each group's performance, you may wish to have a representative of the group fill in the notes on the overhead for the class. You may find it helpful to coordinate this activity with your school's music teacher and/or with your English teacher.

2. Draw a T-chart on the board or overhead. As a class, list the positive and negative effects of HEI.

3. Ask students (either in pairs or individually) to rank both the positive and negative effects from one to five, with one being the least serious and five being the most serious.

4. Lead a class discussion answering the central question, "Do the positive effects of HEI outweigh the negative effects? Why or why not?"

HEI Notes

Terracing

Terracing is making _____ into _____ for farming. They are created by _____. Terraces are found throughout _____. They affect the environment by changing the _____ and by preventing _____ _. Terraces affect people by providing _____, and therefore, more _____.

Desertification

Desertification is the spread of _____. It is caused by _____ and _____. The biggest example of desertification is the _____ in Africa. It is also found in Asia, south of the _____. Desertification affects the environment by destroying _____ and causing _____. It affects people by decreasing _____ and _____ _____ areas, which decrease people's incomes.

Polders

Polders are land that used to be _____. They are built by _____. Polders are found mainly in _____, in western Europe. They affect the environment by creating _____ _____ and by destroying _____. They affect people by creating more _____ for _____ and _____ _____.

HEI Notes *(cont.)*

Pollution

Pollution is the _____ of the _____

_____. _____ cause pollution. The two biggest causes of pollution

are the growth of _____ and burning _____ fuels.

Pollution is found _____, but especially in large cities, such

as _____, and at _____ disaster sites, like

Chernobyl. Pollution contributes to _____, destroys plants

and _____, and contaminates _____, __

_____, and _____. It can cause _____

_____ and _____ in people, and it destroys

sources of _____ and _____.

Deforestation

Deforestation is the _____.

_____, cattle ranching, _____, and the need

for firewood all cause deforestation. Deforestation is mainly an issue for

_____ all over the world, especially in _____,

Malaysia, and Nepal. Deforestation causes a build-up of _____

_____ in the atmosphere, the _____ of topsoil,

and the destruction of natural _____. It affects people by

_____ the greenhouse effect and by destroying _____

____ and _____ sources found only in the rainforest.

Terracing

Terracing is the process of making hills or mountains into steps in order to produce more farmland. Terraces look like large, flat steps carved into mountains and hills. People create terraces in areas where there are a lot of mountains. People adapt to these mountainous areas by creating terraces on which they can farm. Terraces are especially useful for crops that require a lot of water, such as rice. Rice is grown in "paddies," or flooded fields. If the paddies were put on mountains, the water would wash away, leaving the rice shoots too dry to grow.

Terracing is found throughout China and Southeast Asia. These areas depend on rice crops for food, and they are too mountainous to grow rice without terraces.

Terracing affects the environment by changing the physical landscape. Instead of mountains and hills, terraced land looks like huge, shallow steps. In addition, it provides human beings with more crops, which provide both food and money. Terracing also cuts down on the erosion of topsoil.

Courtesy of www.photos.com

Text adapted from *World Geography Today*

Desertification

Desertification is the expansion of desert into areas that were not deserts before. This occurs normally over long periods of time, but human beings have sped up desertification in recent years. Overgrazing of vegetation by livestock exposes topsoil, which then erodes (wears away). Overgrazing happens when ranchers feed their herds on the same land over and over. Farming also increases the pace of desertification. Clearing land to plant crops exposes topsoil, which erodes with wind and precipitation.

Desertification occurs wherever there are deserts and people. The areas that are most affected by desertification are the Sahel, south of the Sahara Desert in North Africa, and the area surrounding the southern Gobi Desert in China.

Desertification also destroys other types of vegetation regions. For example, there used to be large forests in the Sudan. Now, there is desert. In addition, desertification is destroying the rainforest around Lake Chad on the southern edge of the Sahel. Desertification decreases available farmland and, therefore, decreases food and income sources for local residents. In addition, as desertification increases with overgrazing, ranchers need to move their cattle and other livestock to new areas for grazing, causing the spread of desertification over larger areas.

Courtesy of www.clipart.com

Text adapted from *World Geography Today*

Polders

Polders are lands that have been reclaimed from the sea. The land was originally covered by seawater but has been made dry enough to be arable (farm-able). People in low-lying areas, like the Netherlands, have been building polders for years. Building polders is a complicated process, but there are two basic steps. The first step is to build a wall along the shoreline. Second, the water is pumped out using windmills. The result is land that is dry enough to farm and build houses on.

Polders are found in the Netherlands. The Netherlands is one of the Low Countries of Europe. These countries are called Low Countries because of their location below sea level. You can see how important it is in a country that is more than 25% below sea level to create more opportunities for farming and housing.

Polders affect the environment by moving seawater out of an area, creating more dry land. This affects human populations by giving them more space to build houses, and eventually cities, and by providing more farmland. All of these results allow people to have more food and more money. However, building polders also destroys underwater habitats. At this point, polders are very limited and do not have a huge impact on underwater species worldwide.

Courtesy of www.clipart.com

Text adapted from *World Geography Today*

Pollution

Pollution is the contamination of the environment. Air, water, and land can all be polluted. Some places have become so polluted that they are uninhabitable (people cannot live there). Pollution destroys whole species of plants and animals. Pollution has become a bigger problem as population and industry have grown. As populations increase, more garbage and waste are produced. More people mean more cars, which burn fossil fuels (coal and oil). Industries also contribute to pollution by burning fossil fuels and by dumping hazardous waste and sewage.

Pollution is a problem all over the globe. Major urban areas, such as Mexico City, contain much pollution. Nuclear disaster sites such as Chernobyl in the Ukraine have concentrated amounts of pollution. Oil spills, such as the one caused by the Exxon Valdez off the coast of Alaska, also contribute to global pollution.

Pollution affects the environment in many ways. Air pollution destroys the ozone layer, which contributes to the greenhouse effect. It also produces acid rain (polluted rain water). Water and land pollution destroy habitats for hundreds of species of plants and animals. These results affect human beings. The greenhouse effect contributes to global warming, which in turn contributes to rising water levels, which means that available land is shrinking. In addition, polluting land and water destroys food sources. Many governments throughout the world have begun to work together to help slow down pollution.

Courtesy of www.clipart.com

Text adapted from *World Geography Today*

Deforestation

Deforestation means cutting down and removing trees from a forest. There are four main causes of deforestation. Farming and cattle ranching are two reasons for deforestation. Many people clear-cut areas of rainforest in order to grow crops for their families. However, rainforest land has poor soil, and these farms can only survive for about three years. When the land can no longer grow crops, these farmers must clear-cut more land. Cattle ranchers often take over the old farmland for grazing their cows. Cattle can eat many acres a day. Industry is another reason for deforestation. The demand for wood and paper products has increased in many countries, causing a lot of the deforestation in developed countries. In developing countries, forestland is often cut for firewood to heat homes and cook food.

Deforestation is found in all of the major rainforest areas of the world. As you already know, these areas are found nearest the equator. Nepal, Brazil, and Malaysia have the largest deforestation problems in the world.

Deforestation has increased Earth's carbon dioxide levels. More carbon dioxide means a bigger greenhouse effect, which is responsible for global warming. Deforestation has also made large portions of Earth's farmland un-arable (unfarmable). Trees hold topsoil in place. Without trees, the land can be eroded and floods can occur. Finally, deforestation has wiped out many species of plants and animals.

Courtesy of www.clipart.com

Text adapted from *World Geography Today*

Rap Directions

Directions: Your group will work together to create a rap lyric explaining one form of human-environment interaction (HEI). Rap songs use many types of rhyme. Below are some examples of these different types of rhyme that you can use in your lyrics.

End Rhyme: The ends of each line rhyme. They can be next to each other, or they can alternate.

I like rice. (A)	I like rice (A)
It's very nice (A)	With my peas. (B)
With my peas (B)	It's very nice (A)
Or in my teas. (B)	In my teas. (B)

Internal Rhyme: rhymes within a single line

I like rice because it's nice.

I like it in teas, and I like it with peas.

Alliteration: repetition of a consonant or a vowel sound, usually within a single line. However, it can be carried into other lines. Alliteration does not have to come at the beginning of each word.

I like nice rice.

I **m**ight **m**ake **m**ore to**m**orrow.

Directions for creating a rap lyric:

1. Read your information sheet as a group.

2. Fill in the corresponding section of your notes.

3. Use your notes to create four to six lines of a rap that includes the main ideas in your notes.

4. Practice your rap several times to get comfortable performing it.

HEI Notes Key

Terracing

Terracing is making *hills or mountains* into *flat steps* for farming. They are created by *people*. Terraces are found throughout *East and Southeast Asia*. They affect the environment by changing the *landscape* and by preventing *erosion*. Terraces affect people by providing *more food*, and therefore, more *money*.

Desertification

Desertification is the spread of *deserts*. It is caused by *farming* and *overgrazing*. The biggest example of desertification is the *Sahel* in Africa. It is also found in Asia, south of the *Gobi Desert*. Desertification affects the environment by destroying *vegetation* and causing *erosion*. It affects people by decreasing *farming* and *grazing* areas, which decrease people's income.

Polders

Polders are land that used to be *under water*. They are built by *people*. Polders are found mainly in *the Netherlands*, in western Europe. They affect the environment by creating *more dry land*, and by destroying *underwater habitats*. They affect people by creating more *land* for *housing* and *farming*.

Pollution

Pollution is the *contamination* of the *environment*. *People* cause pollution. The two biggest causes of pollution are the growth of *industries*, and burning *fossil* fuels. Pollution is found *everywhere*, but especially in large cities, such as *Mexico City*, and at *nuclear* disaster sites, like Chernobyl. Pollution contributes to *global warming*, destroys plants and *animals*, and contaminates *air, water,* and *soil*. It can cause *sickness* and *birth defects* in people, and it destroys sources of *food* and *medicine*.

Deforestation

Deforestation is the *destruction of forests*. *Farming*, cattle ranching, *industry*, and the need for firewood all cause deforestation. Deforestation is mainly an issue for *rainforests* all over the world, especially in *Brazil*, Malaysia, and Nepal. Deforestation causes a build-up of *carbon dioxide* in the atmosphere, the *erosion* of topsoil, and the destruction of natural *habitats*. It affects people by *increasing* the greenhouse effect, and by destroying *food* and *medicine* sources found only in the rainforest.

Countries, They're GRRRReat!

Overview

In this final project, students create cereal boxes advertising the countries of their choice, using principles of advertising art and the skills from this series. Their projects will reflect the physical and cultural geography of their chosen countries.

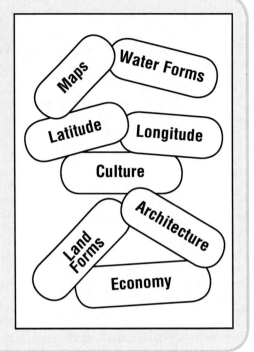

Objective

- Students will understand the physical and human characteristics of a place.

Central Question

What are the physical and human characteristics of a specific geographical place?

Materials

You will need to prepare and/or provide the following:

- cereal boxes or other boxes of similar size (one per student)
- tape, glue, scissors
- crayons/markers
- colored paper

- unlined paper for sketches
- *Project Directions* (one per student), page 169
- overhead transparency of *Project Directions*
- *Rubric* (one per student), page 170
- *Design Sketches* (one set per student), pages 171–173

Countries, They're GRRRReat! *(cont.)*

Directions

1. Before you are ready to begin the project, ask your students to bring in empty cereal boxes or other boxes of a similar size.

2. Distribute the boxes to your students.

3. Ask your students to brainstorm words that describe how the boxes are decorated (look for suggestions such as *bright*, *colorful*, *eye-catching*, *logos*, *trademarked characters*) and what information is found on the box (what it is, how it's good for you, prize inside, etc.).

4. Explain to your students that cereal companies hire marketing people to generate their box designs. It is the marketing artist's job to create cover art that entices shoppers to buy the product.

5. Public art has become a major marketing tool, used to increase civic pride and increase tourism. Campaigns such as "Salmon in the City" (Salem, Oregon), "Dinos on Parade" (Elgin, Illinois), and "A Horse Affair 2005" (Manchester, Vermont) have sprung up all over the country. This project aims to expand on that idea. Tell your students that they have been hired by specific countries of the world to be their marketing artists. Each student's job is to entice tourists to come to the country he or she chose. But, their ads will be displayed on cereal boxes, rather than on street corners.

6. Display *Project Directions* on the overhead projector and go over them with your students. You may wish to have the students submit their design sketches (see the final element in *Project Directions*) to you for approval and/or suggestions before they begin construction of the cereal boxes.

7. You may wish to cover the boxes as a class, since all students may not know how to wrap a present. Thin colored paper or contact paper works best, but construction paper works well, too.

8. Create your own public art display by arranging the finished boxes in a prominent area of your school or by placing them strategically throughout the building. You may find it helpful to coordinate this project with your school's art teacher.

Project Directions

Congratulations! You have been hired by _____ *(name of country)* to head up their newest marketing campaign, "Countries, They're GRRRReat!" You will be the lead marketing artist in charge of creating a cereal box that advertises _____'s physical and cultural geography. Your design must include the following elements:

- Name of your country

- Map of your country (Don't forget to include all of the map components—title, compass rose, scale, legend or key.)

- Three major land or water forms

- Capital city and its latitude and longitude

- Description of your country's climate (Bonus: create a climate graph!)

- Effects of plate tectonics on your country (mountains, earthquakes, etc.)

- Example of your country's architecture (Explain how the example relates to the country's physical geography.)

- Three major imports (Name at least one resource that your country lacks, based on its imports.)

- Three major exports and the natural resources they come from

- Example of HEI and its effects

- Description of your country's political system

- Any natural disasters that your country faces (Bonus: How do people in your country prepare for natural disasters?)

- Cultural identity (What are the major cultural groups in your country? How well do they get along with one another?)

- Water issues (What issues does your country face in terms of water conservation/use? Bonus: Offer a solution.)

- Before assembling your cereal box, use three pages of blank, unlined paper as design sketches—one for the front, one for the back, and one for the sides of the box—showing how and where the information above will appear on the cereal box itself.

Rubric

You have received a grade for your cereal box based on the following:

- Map of your country   _____ of _____ points
- Three major land or water forms   _____ of _____ points
- Capital city and its latitude and longitude   _____ of _____ points
- Description of your country's climate   _____ of _____ points
- Effects of plate tectonics on your country   _____ of _____ points
- Example of your country's architecture   _____ of _____ points
- Explanation of how architecture relates to your country's physical geography   _____ of _____ points
- Three major imports and missing resource   _____ of _____ points
- Three major exports and natural resources   _____ of _____ points
- HEI and its effects   _____ of _____ points
- Description of your country's political system   _____ of _____ points
- Any natural disasters your country faces   _____ of _____ points
- Cultural identity   _____ of _____ points
- Water issues   _____ of _____ points
- Advertising art principles   _____ of _____ points
- Other: _____   _____ of _____ points

                                TOTAL: _____ of _____ points

Comments:

Design Sketch: Front

Use the space below to sketch your design for the front of the cereal box.

Design Sketch: Back

Use the space below to sketch your design for the back of the cereal box.

Design Sketch: Sides

Use the spaces below to sketch your design for the sides of the cereal box.

How to Group Students

Most of the activities in this book require group work. Instead of having students simply count off to create groups, try one of these methods. Students will have more fun getting into groups and will benefit from working with a variety of classmates. You'll have more fun creating groups, too.

- Distribute randomly shuffled playing cards as your students enter the room. Then, use either the suits or the numbers to group your students.

- Assign each student a country or let your students choose countries. Group them by continent or by region. Use continents only if you need fewer than five groups. (Australia and Antarctica really don't lend themselves to this method.)

- Group your students by the month of their birthday. If you have a large group for one or two months, use the dates to create smaller groups.

- Group your students by the time they wake up in the morning or the time they go to bed at night.

- Use the last two digits of your students' phone numbers to group them. You could either create groups with all of the numerals between zero and nine (or fewer, if needed), or you could create groups with the same numbers, such as all of the twenties in one group, all of the thirties in another.

- A twist on the old favorite—group your students alphabetically by their first names instead of their last names.

- Group your students by the number of siblings in their families.

- Take advantage of your students' fashion sense, and use an article of clothing to group students. For example, you could use the color of their shirts to make groups.

- Students' shoe sizes can be used to make groups.

Group Roles

After forming groups, you may wish to assign each group member a role. This practice can help students work together efficiently and cooperatively. You can capitalize on different students' strengths and make their groups more productive.

• Recorder
• Presenter
• Artist
• Designer
• Research Coordinator
• Editor
• Paraphrasing Specialist
• Spell Checker
• Grammar Checker
• Timekeeper
• Diplomat to Other Groups
• Topic Expert
• Mapping Coordinator
• Rhythm Section
• Scavenger
• Accountant
• Interrogator
• Summarizer
• Actor
• Director
• Prop Master
• Playwright
• Musician

Incentive Suggestions

Several of the activities in this book require the use of some kind of incentive. Incentives do not have to be material rewards, although they certainly can be. Below are some suggestions for incentives with which you can encourage your students as they explore world geography.

- Bonus points on a test or project

- No homework pass

- Lunch with the teacher

- Movie tickets

- Library pass

- Computer time

- Choice of free-time activity

- Stickers

- Stamps

- Grab bag or treasure chest

- School supplies

- Extra recess

- Call home

- Name in the school or class newsletter

- Display work

- Student of the month/week/day

- Note to parents